KNOCKING FOOD OFF ITS PEDESTAL

Eating Your Way to Divine Healing and
Supernatural Health

*Enough of Man's Knowledge
+ Earthly Wisdom!*

TONY MYERS

*Phil 3:19 Their end is
Destruction whose god is
their stomach; their glory is
in their shame, who mind
earthly things.*

EDITOR: Tess Sainz

COVER DESIGNER: Zakaria Nada

Dedication and Acknowledgements

This book is dedicated to all who have supported me in ministry and in contributing to my writing. As always, I can't but help to mention the Jamersons, John and Diana, who are very dear friends. Their encouraging words, working behind the scenes with my website, newsletters and so much more. Tess Sainz whose friendship and devotion to using the English Language properly is a huge asset. Her devotion to my books and correcting my massacring the English Language is off the charts. Oleg Aristo who I lean on for his scriptural knowledge and for a double check on my accurate use of scripture.

To my new church family, thanks for accepting me as I am. I have never had that within the four walls of a church. It is truly refreshing. Those of you who are a part of my Facebook family, I truly appreciate the love and support you've shown me throughout the years. There is an army rising up who, throughout their daily lives, have the courage to witness to others the Love of Christ, show that the Loving Heavenly Father wants us all to live healthy lives, and take the truth of healing, love, and blessings outside the four walls wherever they find themselves. They look for no recognition or honors. They just share the Love of Christ out of a true love for others.

Those who are still seeking to recognize and acknowledge their own healing, my books are for you. Keep seeking, keep knocking, never ever give up. Your healing is always attainable even if it doesn't appear to be that way. The more we persevere and stand on the truth, the more of it we receive. I know the challenges you are going through, struggling to understand the things of God. My own healing and the wisdom of understanding that the Holy Spirit has enlightened me with hasn't come easily or without cost. Be encouraged because the Heavenly Father is a giver and gives abundantly. Indeed, He's already granted us everything that we need, if only we come to believe that. Be Blessed, Be Healed and Be a Blessing.

Table of Contents

Foreword

Pastoring for over 40 years, we have seen miracles of all types throughout my ministry from salvation to cancer being healed. We have worked with the homeless and have seen deliverances from the bondage of sin.

I have read Tony's books and enjoyed his honesty and straightforwardness that he provides in his writing. He is not afraid to tackle the issue he is writing about head on and provide information to provoke thought and change in the reader as well as himself.

Tony writes from a place of experience and provides a view from someone who has walked this path. Not only does Tony write from experience, but also, he provides scriptural reference, and what better reference to have than the Word of God?

In this book, Tony addresses food and its connection to our health. Tony takes us on a journey with an open mind and heart to view food and health and the roles each play in our life. We are reminded that we first are spiritual beings living in a physical world and the Holy Spirit is well able to sustain us.

Let Tony take you on this journey to evaluate what position food has in your life.

~ Bill Chapman
Pastor, House of God Worship Center

Preface

In writing this book, it's been quite the journey. The content within these pages contain years of personal study, prayers, and seeking the wisdom of Holy Spirit. Hand in hand with those things have been experiences, and, yes, many up and downs, but always moving forward and learning. This book has been in the making since before my healing because of my experiences during that time period. After my healing, and as I listened to other believers, it became more evident to me the huge need in the body of Christ for someone to stand up and say, "Wait a minute! There is a better way."

I've seen both extremes when it comes to diet and Christian beliefs. The prevalent one is to watch everything that you put into your mouths because you are responsible for your health. This creates fear whether recognized as such or not. From birth, it's driven into us that food can be the healer or the reason for sickness. After years of believing this way, putting food, medicine, and drink in its proper place will take time and a renewing of the mind to truth. Persevere through it and what you will find is a freedom that you've never experienced before, and not only freedom, but a balance. Everything has to start somewhere and this book is a starting point.

The other side of the same coin is those who believe they can just go hog wild and not care at all. I am free to eat whatever it is I desire, but with that freedom comes a balance because my reliance on Holy Spirit has become the focus. The end goal is not to drink two large bottles of soda a day, eat bags of candy, pounds of bacon, or to prove that I'm so holy I can eat ridiculous portions of food. I've seen this played out, people bragging about being gluttonous. I've even seen people purposely eating and encouraging others to eat food that's been sitting out for days and is obviously spoiled. That, my dear friends, is not walking in the spirit. Especially when you may have the expectation to eat it and not become sick, but what about the others? If they are not at that point of expectation, they eat it, and become violently ill, that isn't love or walking in the spirit. That isn't leading a Spirit led life.

The end goal should be a stronger relationship with Holy Spirit to the point that food is no longer a priority in life. When truly leading a spirit led life, there is a balance, and that balance will happen as a true relationship grows. Can I eat anything I want without it affecting my health? Yes, but why would I want to? True Holiness isn't found in food, it's found in the Spirit of Christ in us.

Within believers there should be no food allergies or diseases caused from food or drink. Reaching that point, the truth must be spoken, but with a balance. I do not worry when there's a massive food recall, but at the same time, I wouldn't encourage another person to consume the food that has been recalled. Balance, my friends, balance.

In writing this book, Holy Spirit has had me push the boundaries of our thinking, of what truly is possible to achieve with Him. But the key is with Him. Without a true relationship and a renewing of the mind, the end results could be disastrous. We can have a way of thinking that we are believing when we truly aren't, when we haven't spent the time cultivating our belief into a true heart belief.

One reading through of this book won't be enough, it is simply a starting point. It must be put so deep into your being that, as you do things, there is no fear. Where fear is involved, that isn't God. Where there is doubt or questioning, then the belief isn't deep enough. Be honest with yourself but spend the time to develop a pure heart belief. Then the miraculous will start to happen. God Bless!

Disclaimer: Read This!

Let it be known that I am not a doctor or in the medical field. I am not recommending any specific diet whatsoever. Anything in this book that may categorize a certain food as healthy or not healthy is strictly my opinion, not to be taken as a medical fact. This book is a study on how God views food and a philosophical discussion on how a believer can change their perspective on food while maintaining their present diet. The health and safety of the readers are of the utmost importance, so be wise.

I do have strong convictions on food and I do express this in writing this book. However, in no way is it my intention to make the reader feel condemned. It is just meant to provoke thought. If you are under a doctor's care, check with your doctor before making any adjustments to your diet.

I also talk about fasting. Once again, your well-being is of the utmost importance. I strongly urge the reader to consult a doctor before going on a fast. Also, in recounting my experiences with fasting, I am in no way trying to encourage the reader to do the same. If your doctor approves going on a fast, take the professional recommendation on how to fast and safely come off the fast as well.

In other areas of the book, I tell how persons that I have ministered to made a choice to eat foods they were once allergic to. These were decisions made by them of their own free will. As I make clear in the accounts of these situations, I recommend that the reader take the advice of their medical professionals and take no unnecessary risks to their health.

With these warnings, it is the reader who is responsible for the choices they make. So, choose wisely. Your life is precious to me, so please act responsibly, taking any and all cautions that a sound mind would dictate. At various times throughout the book, I will remind you of this disclaimer.~ Tony Myers

1: Been There. Done That. Got the T-Shirt.

An open heart and an open mind is asked of you while reading this book. Now, set aside your lifetime of experiences. Let's throw our cards on the table. This topic of food and diet is a toxic subject. Your lifelong beliefs will come into play and you may even wish to set this book down, labeling me as a heretic. The ultimate goal of this book is not to change your diet, but to change your perspective and beliefs about food so you can use food to attain divine health and healing.

The common perception is, when a person is healed, then it's life happily ever after. Actually, when a person is healed, people tend to ignore the years of suffering a person had gone through, much less even consider hardships that come about because of a miraculous healing. Consider a few things like going on social security disability and then trying to find a job.

I had been incapacitated for six years. The first thing SSD wants to do is make accusations of fraud and threaten with having to pay back what had been paid out. Once that is disproven, you're put on a back to work program. They will pay out benefits according to what you earn. That is, once you find a job. Try going to a job interview and explaining a six-year gap in your work history. Aha! You hadn't thought of that, had you?

In my case, I refused to hold back my testimony. So, I would tell them the truth: that I had been healed of ALS by Jesus. Exactly. There are always a variety of reactions. The end result would always be thanks, but no thanks.

The common concern was that the employer would be worried about a relapse. I did find a job. Once working, you have so many months before the cash payments stop depending upon your income at the job. Once the cash benefits stop, you're still considered on SSD, so they start charging you $400.00 a month for their medical insurance (even though I'm a veteran). Every few months, they would state that they overpaid me and want the cash benefits back. This is while I wasn't presently receiving cash benefits. Do you get the picture? There's a reason I'm telling you parts of my 'after the miracle' sob story. It's not for pity. I need a refill of my coffee. Be patient, please.

While all of that is going on, remember, I was a brand-new Believer. There was no mentor or spiritual leader in my life. I'm not gonna go into how I was treated by the church my wife and I had been attending when I was healed. Things with them might have been different if the healing had occurred at the church. I don't know.

Our residence is in my wife's hometown. I had just moved to it when the ALS hit me. Therefore, I was a perfect stranger to the town folk. Directly after my healing, I was walking on cloud number nine. I knew that might end. The Holy Spirit (before I knew about him) was putting it into my heart that I had to learn about this new walk of mine. Really having a relationship with Him was going to be vital.

Prior to the ALS, I had been an atheist, addicted to drugs, alcohol, had PTSD, and was diagnosed as being a Schizoid (Read "The Lord Jesus Healed Me"). I had no clue what normality was. Part of my healing was being delivered of all these things. What I received was the whole package: being saved, healed, delivered (from I'm sure thousands of demons), set free, and made whole. My thinking and thoughts were changed, completely different than I had ever experienced before. I actually had a sound mind for the first time in my life. Yet, Holy Spirit was showing me I had to rely on Him or I would return back to my previous state. In churchy, religious terminology, I had to renew my mind to Truth.

All I had to teach me was scripture and Holy Spirit. Honestly, the thought never occurred to me to go online and find videos of preachers, which I'm thankful for. My wife had Christian channels on all the time, but never did the desire to listen to them enter my heart. For a year and a half when I wasn't praying for the sick, I was studying scripture. It took me that long to finally get a job. Meanwhile, life was still moving forward. My past life was filled with finding comfort in things that we put in our mouths: namely drugs, alcohol, and yes, some would say food (I was junk food junkie), in churchy terms, things of the flesh. I totally dislike that terminology. It is ill-defined. Guess what? I'm renaming it. What you say is fleshly, I use the term what enters in through the physical senses. My skin crawls when I hear someone say, "Oh, forgive me. I was just being fleshly." While we're at it, I'm renaming the carnal mind as well. The carnal mind is the brain, which is the control center of the physical senses. With that settled, not everything that comes in through the physical senses is evil, which when using the term flesh and carnal, that is how it is used.

Since my past is so checkered, I, like most people, had to learn how to overcome the lusts of the physical senses. Rather, how not to fall into the many traps there are. The lusts of the physical senses is when the physical things of this world control us. Better yet, it is when we rely on our physical senses rather than Holy Spirit.

We then have a choice. We are either walking in the spirit or by our physical senses. In order to be healed, we must rely on the Holy Spirit rather than relying on our physical senses. This is the biggest hurdle to overcome when it comes to healing. We feel symptoms, therefore, we *believe* we're still sick. The way that Holy Spirit guided me to learning how to walk in the spirit (to rely on him), was by overcoming the control that food, drink, and drugs had on me in the past.

Things that we ingest have the greatest control over us because they change the way our bodies feel. We seek after those things which make us feel good. When we rely on a physical substance, it isn't lasting. Then, we become addicted to that substance to control how we feel. Our perception of food is the root of relying on the physical senses because we think we need it to sustain us. What we eat or don't eat controls how we feel or how healthy we are. After all, we need it to survive, right? I'm living, breathing proof that is wrong. Otherwise, I wouldn't be typing. I'd be in the graveyard pushing up daisies.

As I'm saying that, I'm not saying that we strive to do away with food. That we deprive our bodies of that substance. Not at all. The Father gave us food to enjoy, changing our perspective that, when we rely on the Holy Spirit, then food doesn't have the power to control our health. Rather, only the Holy Spirit has that power. As we're learning this when it comes to food, the control of everything else easily slips away. We are then able to acknowledge what was difficult to acknowledge before: That we are healed, whole, and healthy through Holy Spirit in us.

First, I'm going to guide you through what brought me to the beliefs of what I'm sharing with you. Indeed, the first six chapters of this book are to expand your thinking. Then, I'll walk you through, so you can see that I'm only talking about a renewing of the mind, not some radical, foolish new way of eating or punishing the "flesh" type of deal.

> *All things are lawful unto me, but all things are not expedient: all things are lawful for me, but I will not be brought under the power of any. (1 Corinthians 6:12, KJV)*

One day early on, I came upon the above verse in Corinthians. Taken out of context or even shortened, it can be used to promote sin. That of course is not Paul's intent. As I was reading this, the next verse caught my eye.

> *Meats for the belly, and the belly for meats: but God shall destroy both it and them…. (1 Corinthians 6:13, KJV)*

Meats in the King James Version means food. This got me thinking and researching. There were two thoughts implanted in my spirit. The first thought is how Paul is dismissing the importance of food. It occurred to me that it was much the same as Jesus stating that what goes into the mouth merely goes out of the body and doesn't reach the heart, so it doesn't defile the man.

The second thought was that all things are lawful for me, but I shall not be brought under the power of any. *Food is* for the belly. I saw this which is what got me thinking. I'm now going to write this the way I saw it so my point is clear. *I shall not be brought under the power of any food.* This got me to thinking how much food controls our lives.

We obsess over it, whether it's by overeating or by over controlling what we eat. There are the two extremes. Yet, they are the same thing. We've given power over to a physical substance and both are obsessions of the same thing, causing worry and fear.

I did an exhaustive search for anything in the scriptures that promotes food as being essential in maintaining health and couldn't find one. And does God hold us accountable for what we eat? Are you so sure of that? The Father refers to the physical substance for comparison so that we can understand and be led to the truth. For instance:

A merry heart doeth good like a medicine: but a broken spirit drieth the bones. (Proverbs 17: 22, KJV)

It isn't saying to take medicine to be healed. In fact, it's saying the opposite. A merry heart is the same as medicine. In other words, a merry heart heals the body and a broken spirit dries up the bones. A broken spirit literally does dry up the bones. Science is proving this is true in the literal, physical sense. If you have a physical ailment, take the medicine of the Lord which is the Joy of the Holy Spirit. Yet, nowhere in scriptures does the Holy Spirit point to food being used to heal. Then, the fateful day of the stomach incident happened, which totally changed my perspective.

This would've been around August 2012. I was set to give my testimony to a group of people. The night right before this, I had intense stomach pain, did not sleep at all, and was curled up on the floor all night in agony. I kept thinking, *"What did I eat* to cause this?" There had to be something that *I did wrong* for this to be happening (pay attention to that).

The night hours creeped by, enveloped in intense pain. Remember, this is coming from a man who had just gone through six years of hell. When I wrote intense pain, that's exactly what it was. I canceled the engagement, ashamed and embarrassed. I had let God down by eating wrong.

Suddenly, Holy Spirit stirred up inside of me, "You were just healed from a terminal illness. Yet, a little tummy ache is keeping you down, stopping you from declaring the works of the Lord. Is a stomach more powerful than me?" I started praising the Lord. The pain left, and I went on to give my testimony.

That was the start of me realizing how much power we give food over our lives. My healing journey and learning how to rely on Holy Spirit has walked hand in hand with overcoming human wisdom, separating what is human knowledge from God's Wisdom.

This didn't happen overnight. What I am sharing with you has been years of seeking Holy Spirit's guidance and having an open heart. There have been many times that I didn't even realize at the time what I was learning. I still have a long way to go, as do we all, but the end goal is to look like Christ. He moved about in the physical world but was unaffected by it. The physical world didn't change Him. He changed the physical world wherever He ventured.

I remember a particular fast that I went on. My job was driving people to their medical appointments. We are talking about driving anywhere from eight hours to fourteen hours. One morning around day twelve, I got out of bed and was so weak that I was on the floor dizzy and lightheaded. I couldn't even get back up. Deb was like, "You gotta eat!" My thoughts went to the other fasts that had ended up poorly, quitting them before the number of days was completed.

Breaking my vow to the Father, feeling ashamed, weak, and condemned, my thoughts were on not breaking my promise again. "Holy Spirit you gotta give me some strength." All of a sudden, I was able to slowly get up. Over a period of a half hour, my head cleared up.

As I was driving that day, I was contemplating what had happened. The fact that I had even gotten to work was a miracle. The scripture, "...in your weakness I am strong," came to my mind. For the rest of that fast, whenever the weakness, foggy mind, and dizziness would come, then I would recall that verse and ask the Holy Spirit's help. At the time, I didn't recognize the significance of this event or that this was the first step in relying on Holy Spirit for all things.

The next event happened months after that fast. I was woken up with my stomach being nauseous and was very weak. It was Christmas Eve. I was supposed to work even though I wasn't in the condition to drive. I was determined to work. After only thirty minutes of driving, I had to call the boss and tell her that it wasn't safe for me to drive. The man who was healed from Lou Gehrig's disease was sick!

Once again, I felt condemned as if I were letting God and Jesus down. The thought of duplicating what I had learned from my last fast didn't even enter my mind. All my thoughts were on that I was a disappointment to my Father. I passed out in bed, woke up, read a verse in scripture, and was contemplating on that verse. Passed out again, woke up, and got a phone call that our vehicle had finally been repaired, ready to be picked.

We had been fighting with a dealership over this vehicle since it had been excessively using up oil. They had refused to repair it under warranty. This had been a month's long battle. We were going to pick it up no matter what. I was still in very bad condition, but very determined to get it.

The dealership was over an hour away. My wife went with me as I was in no condition to drive. When we got there, I had to be the one to deal with the situation. They were claiming to have totally rebuilt the engine in less than a day. I didn't believe it. But I somehow had to come up with the strength to deal with those people. I somewhat absent mindedly stated to my wife that the Lord would just have to help me, not even really believing that He would.

Well we made it through that. Still feeling terrible, we got home, and I went back to bed. The next morning, I woke up angry, still feeling bad. "Enough is enough! Holy Spirit give me strength." That day, I was back to good health.

The purpose of me recounting these events is to show how learning this has been a process and has taken a concerted effort on my part to learn these things. It has been a constant renewing of the mind, the way I thought versus the way the mind of Christ within me thinks. It has been a constant up and down. But with each step and circumstance, I have learned more and more. The Lord is neither hiding nor withholding anything. We have access to all his wisdom now. It's a matter of how quickly we recognize it. Many people think that my knowledge was just miraculously put into me and came about easily. It didn't. I had to seek, knock, then seek and knock some more. I had to have an open heart, willing to embrace what seemed ridiculous. Remembering what the Lord had done in the past was an essential part of the process as well.

For instance, my being sustained for six months while my stomach was paralyzed has been instrumental in the Lord showing me the truths about food and how healing works. Looking back at the other examples, He's used them as well to show me truths. Because of this, you don't have to start at ground zero, but are given a boost when receiving the truths into your heart that I'm sharing.

Another example while learning that food is neutral and shouldn't affect my body in a negative way, I accidentally hit my knee with a sledgehammer, full force, straight on. Therefore, since the giant, food, was crumbling, it was easier to believe that impacting my knee with a sledgehammer should have no ill-effects. This happened subconsciously. When I was being hit with the sledgehammer. I wasn't thinking that. But how I was overcoming my physical senses where it concerned food was making an impact in other areas of life's circumstances. I never even felt pain from the hit, nor did it ever swell or bruise. If it is a heart belief that food is neutral, can I develop acid reflux, gastritis, food poisoning, food allergies, cancer, or the many other diseases that things entering through the mouth are given credit for? The answer is no. If we already have one of those things, then the beginning of this truth will make it easier for you to recognize improvements and be miraculously healed from them.

I had started this journey of learning to rely on Holy Spirit and the fact that food is neutral. At first, having been a junk food junkie (prior to my illness), I did use it as a reason to enable me to indulge in food that is considered unhealthy.

But the more I relied on Holy Spirit, the healthier my diet became without even striving to eat healthier. The reason is because I was having a healthy personal relationship with Holy Spirit. I was relying on him to provide peace, comfort, and His Joy, so I was no longer looking for an outside source to fill those needs.

The more neutral food or anything else is, the weaker the desire to rely on that physical substance for emotional needs. This means that I'm no longer relying on that substance for the positive benefits or negative consequences because Holy Spirit is producing those benefits within me. Now I am trusting Holy Spirit for those needs, not a physical substance. Overeating, bulimia, anorexia, anxiety, alcoholism, all these things can become a thing of the past. An example is that, if I am recognizing that Holy Spirit is removing the pain from my body, then I no longer need a pain pill. I'll take less and less or stop all together.

2: Physical Substances
Take a Knee

The biggest problem with people being healed is the physical senses. Most of us believe that God heals today. Many of us have had healings and seen them in other people. Yet, many are still striving to be able to acknowledge their healing. The reason is being able to recognize that you're healed before the symptoms leave. This is the struggle. It is the struggle of the human body screaming at you, "I'm sick. See? You still feel pain." The struggle lies in your physical senses: what you see, hear, taste, touch, and smell.

In all my other books, I've discussed the control the physical senses have over us. Recognizing this is a first step, how do we overcome our physical senses? That would be the question, my dear friend. The answer for many people will be to overcome the struggle with what goes into our bodies through our mouth.

Throughout this book, I will be focused on food. But really, I'm talking about anything that goes in through the mouth. This includes medicine, liquid substances, and in my case, coffee! Speaking of coffee, let's have some. Hey! I'm not trying to change your diet, so don't try to change mine. Besides, I just saw an article that says coffee drinkers live longer! Of course, I'm joking. My long life comes from Holy Spirit in me.

The key to healing and health is to recognize the lies that the physical world is telling us. The carnal mind, the brain, does indeed mislead us because it doesn't understand that Jesus has redeemed us completely. This includes our bodies when we believe that truth. We've got two minds: the mind of Christ and the mind of Adam (the brain).

The mind of Christ is within our spirit and dictates to us all truth. The mind of Adam dictates to us what is coming in through the physical senses than automatically responds through our bodies. The one that wins is the one we believe. The one that loses is the one that we believe is wrong. The choice resides in our soul. A renewed mind will choose what the mind of Christ is inputting in us. The unrenewed mind will choose what the physical senses are inputting to us and what our brain is automatically reacting to. In either case, what our soul truly believes is deposited in our heart, then our response in this physical realm is in reaction to what our beliefs of the heart are.

The key to living "in the spirit" is to react based on the mind of Christ. This is, once again, based upon what we truly believe in our core being or heart. The beginning process is to make the choice of what our core beliefs are through renewing our mind/soul to the mind of Christ. There is a balance. We must make the decision when to use our physical senses to interact with the physical world and when the mind of Christ is saying, "No, don't react that way." For instance, if driving a car, we must use our physical senses to interact with the physical world. The mind of Christ is in agreement with that. The mind of Christ, however, is never in agreement with the things of death. Anything contrary to life is contrary to the mind of Christ. The balance lies in deciding which things in our physical life are God's Wisdom and which are man's wisdom. The two are rarely in agreement. Here are some scriptures to help make the distinction.

> *I will give you the keys (authority) of the kingdom of heaven; and whatever you bind [forbid, declare to be improper and unlawful] on earth will have [already] been bound in heaven, and whatever you loose [permit, declare lawful] on earth will have [already] been loosed in heaven. (Matthew 16:19, Amplified Bible)*

> *Set your affection on things above, not on things on the earth. (Colossians, 3:2 KJV)*

The deciding factor is then, does the item in question remain in heaven or is it bound in heaven? This is one of the most useful tools to use in determining whose wisdom it is: God's or man's, the mind of Christ or the mind of Adam. Whether the information within these chapters will help you is based on which you choose to believe; your experience or the mind of Christ. If the information is loosed in heaven, then that is the truth whether your experiences stack up to it or not. Your willingness to make your decisions off of these factors is the amount that your life and health will change.

For instance, in heaven, is the health of the person dependent upon what goes in through the mouth? The argument will be that we won't have bodies which would be irrelevant. God's truth is not dependent on whether we are in earthen vessels or not. Because we are spiritual beings first, that is the truth we should be working from. At this point, most of our earthly experiences won't match up to the truth. The key is to work from the truth, not from our experiences. The more truth changes our core beliefs in our hearts, the more we will live out that truth. This can take time and a concerted effort to believe the truth only, and be committed to making these things a core belief.

Why is it that two people can be on the same diet, one will live a long healthy life, and the other will be plagued from disease and fight with health problems throughout their lives? If it were a simple matter of diet, then both people, when eating a healthy diet, would live long and healthy lives. Or how is it that a person who eats an unhealthy diet all their life lives to be a hundred? People who smoke cigarettes outliving those who don't. Rock stars, actors, and actresses from the seventies and eighties who were heavy into drugs, not taking care of themselves at all, are still alive and kicking in their eighties. How are they outliving Christians who believe In Christ and are taking care of their bodies?

Most of us know at least one person that fits the examples above. You are absolutely right! That paragraph was to get your attention. How does a man whose stomach is paralyzed live six months without any sustenance whatsoever? Then, that man goes on to be healed completely from Lou Gehrig's disease. That man would be me just in case you didn't know.

Actually, I fit all the parameters that those rock stars fit as well. Drugs, cigarettes, a junk food diet. Still, I live! This includes at the age of forty-three, I had the worst case of emphysema that the breathing specialist had ever seen. I couldn't take two steps without getting dizzy, struggling to even breathe, or exhale. A, "Thank you, Jesus!" is very appropriate here!

Take note that this author may have some revelation that can be used for your benefit and what the correct beliefs are when it comes to what goes in the mouth. Also, you may find a certain amount of revelation as to what it takes to meet the aspirations of walking in divine health.

When asked what an appropriate diet is, the majority will answer meat, vegetables, fruit, and bread groups in the correct amounts. In order to have the body operate correctly, that is what the requirements are. Feed the machine properly and it will function properly. We are all taught this at an early age. "These types of food are healthy, the rest aren't. Put too much butter on your bread, then your blood will have the wrong type of fats and clogged arteries are the result."

Both our life experiences and the knowledge of the medical professionals show that as the overall truth. Yet, that knowledge is ever changing, and the outcome is never what is expected. We continually try to manage our health through our diet and teach others to do the same. Cancer occurs in people that have taken care of their bodies and eaten properly. This same cancer appears in those who haven't as well. A person that eats chicken and fish may have the same health problems as one who eats pork. Yet, we still look to food to keep us healthy.

We spend thousands of dollars and hundreds of hours researching to find how to best keep our bodies healthy. What we eat is the decider to if we are healthy or unhealthy. What are we then dependent upon to maintain our good health? Therefore, who or what is our god?

Many of us, when we get sick, what is the first thing we do? We jump on the internet to do research. We search to find out what diet or medicines have been successful in treating our current symptoms. Hello! I did that very thing as well. We often rationalize this with, "God made this type of food to heal us." Meanwhile, one food works for one person and apparently not for another.

If God made a certain type of food to heal, if that were the case, since God is no respecter of persons, it would work the same for every person. When food fails us, then we turn to medicine, supplements, or herbs. One doctor will recommend this, that, or the other. Yet, another doctor will recommend other things. One person will state that this herb worked for them, and yet, it doesn't work for another person. What are we relying on for health and healing? We may invoke the name of Jesus. Yet really, who is our healer? What do we give credit to by our actions? What is our expectation in? Awwww! C'mon! You can admit to it. It's food! Let's call a spade a spade.

> *...Whose end is destruction, whose God is their belly, and whose glory is in their shame, who mind earthly things.)* (Philippians 3:19, KJV)

We get a common cold. What's the first reaction? Tea with honey in it, cough medicine, and aspirin. These are our remedies. Are these from God? No rationalizing, "Well, Tony, the Father gave us the knowledge of those things to heal us." No, that is man's wisdom. A person drank tea and honey and they felt better. Then other people tried it and it helped them also. Thus, was born the idea that tea and honey works for a sore throat. This is all earthly knowledge born of the mind of Adam.

Our expectation based on experience states to drink tea with honey and it will relieve the symptoms. Most of the time, the relief is temporary and doesn't last long. We must drink more of it. The best we can do in most cases is to ride it out until the symptoms run their course. Please see the disclaimer if you didn't read it. The disclaimer and clarifier are in there. A little harshness is needed because reliance of what we put in our mouths is so prevalent in our society. These actions I'm describing are accepted at face value. So, it must be confronted head-on.

What is the one thing mankind struggles the most with? That's right, food! Everyone has had struggles with food. Food is the one thing the serpent used to tempt Eve. That is where the struggle with diet started. All throughout scripture we see a struggle with food. Esau sold his birthright over food. God doesn't judge Jacob for blackmailing Esau. He judges Esau for giving his birthright away for food.

> *Lest there be any fornicator, or profane person, as Esau, who for one morsel of meat sold his birthright. (Hebrews 12:16, KJV)*

> *As it is written, Jacob have I loved, but Esau have I hated. (Romans 9:13, KJV)*

> *...thus Esau despised his birthright. (Genesis 25:34, KJV)*

Think about this: Esau is starving to death. Yet, because he placed more importance on food, God hated him! Really ponder this. Esau could've died from starvation. Yet, he is listed as a profane person because of food! If Esau had rejected Jacob's proposal, God would've provided for him.

Cain killed his brother over food. Not only that but Cain held food in such high regard, that he held back from giving God the best of the crop. All throughout scripture we see this played out.

Do you see how mankind since the beginning has made food their god? It isn't any different today. Let me interject that it isn't food that is evil, it's the position we place it in that is evil. I really want this to sink in. We will rationalize this away, "But, *Tony, we need food to live.*" **Go right back up to Esau!**

Food involves every single physical sense: eyesight, touch, taste, smell, and hearing. This is why it is so powerful. When we put food in its proper place, then we will learn to overcome our physical senses. They will no longer have the tight grip that controls our every decision. With healing, that is the key: to overcome our physical senses that are telling us that our body is sick. When we learn to trust God over food, then walking "in the spirit" becomes easier in every single aspect of our lives. This is how we "crucify" the flesh and learn how to put The Father above all things.

When we learn that food should be neutral, that it is Holy Spirit alone that we should trust, it is He who will keep our bodies healthy. Indeed, the very way food is processed today, what food is actually healthy? There isn't a consumable product out there that isn't altered in one way or the other. With fruit and vegetables there are the many pesticides, even in organic farming, and rampant genetic manipulation. With all of the meat group, not only is there the genetic manipulation, but they feed from the ground that has soaked up all the poisons we've dumped into it. With fish, there are polluted waters with mercury levels rising higher and higher with every passing day. Name one meat product that hasn't been the cause of people dying. Yet, many people consider chicken and fish as the best food to eat.

Hopefully, this chapter has provoked you to thought, and has caused you to knock food down from the spot of being a god that has the power of life and death over our bodies. What is a god? A god is something that controls us and has power over our lives. There is only one True God and food isn't it, although we've given it that power.

Before we get to the strategy of how to overcome the power and control that food has in our lives by Trusting God, we will cover how God the Father views food and, if scripturally, is there a diet He would prefer us to have. Many preachers will use the Old Covenant diet, the ceremonially clean and unclean foods, as a claim that the Old Covenant diet is the Divine Diet of God. Along with that, we will look at are if we at fault for our health, and if God judges us for what we put into our bodies.

These things are essential to understanding how to overcome our physical senses and put a working blueprint in place that will help to overcome the many pitfalls of relying on our physical senses in every aspect of our lives. This blueprint, if followed, will bring back the enjoyment of food without the fear attached to it. God wants us to enjoy food and use food as a means to fellowship. He doesn't want it to control us. He wants us to use it to interact with others without fear, stress, and worry!

3: It Always Starts With
The Serpent

The majority of diseases if not all are linked to what goes into our bodies. Therefore, we search scriptures to come up with what the divine diet is. Some say Daniel's fast. Some say the diet under the Old Covenant, that the Jewish diet is where God's heart is. I say that the diet He wants us on is the Bread of Life and He does not have a concern for what goes in the mouth. With that stated, I must prove that. Then we can move forward to transitioning away from the idea that it is food keeping us healthy. But first, let's have us a cup of coffee.

Did you know the best way to taste all the flavors of coffee is by slurping it? For real! So, forgive me while I slurp.

In the garden, God gave Adam and Eve every herb that bears seed, and every tree which has fruit yielding seed. At that time and based solely on the serpent, we could say that animals had a higher level of

ere able to communicate verbally with mankind. I
ere was a higher level of spirituality among the
ll accounts before the fall, all animals dwelt
together. The serpent, if we choose to view the serpent as a
literal animal, knew of God. Look at how many religions view animals
as sacred. There are a number of things after the fall that I look at. God
cursed the serpent as His first reaction to the eating of the fruit.

> *And the Lord God said unto the serpent, Because thou hast
> done this, thou art cursed above all cattle, and above every
> beast of the field; upon thy belly shalt thou go, and dust shalt
> thou eat all the days of thy life: (Genesis 3:14 KJV)*

Then, after the pronouncing of what would happen because of the fruit
being eaten, God made clothes from the skin of an animal. This means
God killed an animal now placing them far lower than man.

I do believe that, because it was an animal that tempted Eve, scriptures
start to show a certain disdain for animals, thereby making them less
than He had created them to be. I do also imagine that this was the first
time that man ate meat. I just don't see God, after making clothes out
of an animal, leaving that animal to rot.

Another eyebrow raiser is the fact that Abel kept sheep. Why was he
raising sheep? Perhaps for clothing and food. God saw Abel's offering
and had respect for the offering and Abel, not for Cain's offering. We
see in Numbers and Leviticus that the sacrifice of the clean animals was
a sweet savor to the Lord. It would appear that man started to eat meat
directly after the fall. God had also already separated all things into

KNOCKING FOOD OFF ITS PEDESTAL

clean and unclean. We see this with Noah. God told him to keep seven of each clean animal and two of the unclean. Remember, this was long before the Law of Moses was enacted.

> *Of every clean beast thou shalt take to thee by sevens, the male and his female: and of beasts that are not clean by two, the male and his female. (Genesis 7:2, KJV)*

In doing so, that would have given Noah and his family enough food to eat until the flood was dried up with enough left over to continue to breed. I am going somewhere with this, I promise you. God did have His reason for all of this, which we will get to. I'm just setting this background up. Here comes the reset button.

The flood waters leave and Noah and all the occupants leave the Ark. The first thing that happens is Noah builds an altar and sacrifices every clean animal to the LORD. After that is completed, He makes the same statement that He had made to Adam and Eve in the beginning.

> *And God blessed Noah and his sons, and said unto them, Be fruitful, and multiply, and replenish the earth. (Genesis 9:1, KJV)*

This could be considered a restarting, in which things would be different. Immediately after that is:

> *And the fear of you and the dread of you shall be upon every beast of the earth, and upon every fowl of the air, upon all that moveth upon the earth, and upon all the fishes of the sea; into your hand are they delivered. Every moving thing that liveth shall be meat for you; even as the green herb have I given you all things. (Genesis 9:2-3, KJV)*

And I will establish my covenant with you; neither shall all flesh be cut off any more by the waters of a flood; neither shall there any more be a flood to destroy the earth. And God said, This is the token of the covenant which I make between me and you and every living creature that is with you, for perpetual generations. (Genesis 9:11-12, KJV)

An explanation is needed here. Where does God link health with food? Really consider this. At this point, the only link to good health and food is the tree of Life. Who is the tree of Life or, another name would be, the Bread of Life? That's right! Jesus. I really want you to ponder this.

In the first nine chapters of the Bible, where is the link to good health? In being attained by what you eat. Later in Genesis, we have Esau exchanging his birthright for food and he becomes despised.

All creatures are declared underneath us and good for consumption. Hold your tongue! You're fixing to bring up the Laws of Moses. We ain't there yet. Let's take a closer look at the Noahic Covenant.

Is that Covenant really just that God will never cause another flood? I don't believe that is the Covenant He's referring to. Notice how God adds, "neither shall all flesh be cut off any more by the waters of a flood." I believe God is actually referencing the New Covenant which is in the far future. That is just food (pun intended) for thought. From this point forward, God is declaring that we can eat all foods, but are forbidden to eat blood or fat. Nowhere is God proclaiming that it is food that will give us a long and healthy life. Prove me wrong!

Abraham, while he was a gentile before the law of Moses, was declared to be the father of our faith. This is how gentiles are included in the promise. Once Jesus fulfilled the Law of Moses, we as gentiles now are descendants of Abraham, therefore, heirs to the promise. In the same manner, with the foreshadowing of the sacrifices and feasts having been fulfilled in Christ, there is now no more need for the food restrictions. The commandment that God gave to Noah, that all creatures are given to us for food, now stands. In fact, for gentiles there was never a change. The commandment God had given to Noah stood throughout the centuries. The restrictions had only been put upon the children of Israel, for a period of time, until Christ fulfilled their purpose.

Then, we get to the Exodus when the children of Israel left Egypt and were in the desert for forty years. Both before the Law of Moses and after Mount Sinai, The Lord provided for them supernaturally even while they were being rebellious. This should be a testimony to us. The loving Father will provide for us even when we aren't acting like His sons and daughters. All we have to do is to believe in His goodness and that He will provide for us.

> *And Moses said, This shall be, when the Lord shall give you in the evening flesh to eat, and in the morning bread to the full;...(Exodus 16:8, KJV)*
>
> *And the children of Israel did eat manna forty years, until they came to a land inhabited; they did eat manna, until they came into the borders of the land of Canaan. (Exodus 16:35, KJV)*
>
> *And Moses said unto Aaron, take a pot, and put an omer*

*full of manna therein, and lay it up before the Lord, to be
kept for your generations. As the Lord commanded Moses,
so Aaron laid it up before the Testimony, to be kept.
(Exodus 16:33-34, KJV)*

There is much significance to the Father providing the manna and quail. Even keeping the omer of manna was to be a reminder that He always provides. The bread from heaven bears a far more significant symbol. Jesus came and declared Himself to be the Bread of Life. Just as He sustained Israel in the desert with bread from heaven, now we have the everlasting bread of life.

With that said, man has placed an importance on food and water that God doesn't. Yes, I know that seems to be an outrageous suggestion. Why does it take such an outcry from the children of Israel for God to act when it comes to things that go in the mouth? Why wasn't Moses saying Lord feed us, that is until the people started murmuring against both Moses and God? If the people were dying of thirst and hunger, Moses would've been as well. Why did it take an outcry from the children of Israel for Moses to act? "Interesting point, Tony." No, I really want you to ponder on this. Once again there is absolutely no clear statements from God that He is reliant upon nutrition to sustain our bodies. Let's look how often they murmured against Moses where it comes to food and water.

*And the people murmured against Moses, saying, What
shall we drink? (Exodus 15:24, KJV)*

*And the whole congregation of the children of Israel
murmured against Moses and Aaron in the wilderness: And*

the children of Israel said unto them, Would to God we had
died by the hand of the Lord in the land of Egypt, when we
sat by the flesh pots, and when we did eat bread to the full;
for ye have brought us forth into the wilderness, to kill this
whole assembly with hunger. (Exodus 16:2-3, KJV)

And the people thirsted there for water; and the people
murmured against Moses, and said, Wherefore is this that
thou hast brought us up out of Egypt, to kill us and our
children and our cattle with thirst? And Moses cried unto
the Lord, saying, What shall I do unto this people? They be
almost ready to stone me. (Exodus 17:3-4, KJV)

It is absolutely my contention that in the desert, God's plan wasn't to sustain them by feeding them. Rather, it was to show them that He could and would sustain them without food or water which is one reason why it would take such an outcry before God acted.

Then Jesus said unto them, Verily, verily, I say unto you,
*Moses **gave you not** that bread from heaven; but my*
Father giveth you the true bread from heaven. For the bread
of God is he which cometh down from heaven, and giveth life
unto the world. (John 6:32-33, KJV)

And the Lord said unto Samuel, Hearken unto the voice of
the people in all that they say unto thee: for they have not
rejected thee, but they have rejected me, that I should not
reign over them. (1 Samuel 8:7, KJV)

Now therefore hearken unto their voice: howbeit yet protest
solemnly unto them, and shew them the manner of the king
that shall reign over them. (1 Samuel 8:9, KJV)

The children of Israel grumbled for a king just as they grumbled for food. God granted them that, even though it wasn't His Will that they have a king. Just as I contend, His intention was to show them He would sustain them without the need for food.

There are many probable reasons that the people got to this point and were willing to turn against a man and God who had already walked them through many dangers. They had already seen God be true in many mighty miracles. Yet, for food and water, they were very willing to turn on both and run back to slavery. Any possible theories we can come up with all show one thing: a willingness to be controlled by what goes in our mouths.

I had questioned why the Israelite's got to the point that they felt they were going to die of starvation or thirst. Moses never mentions himself or Aaron being at that point. The last two instances of thirst were while they were being fed everyday by manna from heaven. Every night, fowls would show up inside the camp that they could eat the meat from. Is it fair to say that the physical substances controlled them and were really what they put into god status? I think yes. We do the very same thing. I also think that, if God delayed providing for them, then it would have been to show them that He would sustain them and He didn't need physical food or water to do so. Proof of this is myself who God sustained for six months while my stomach and throat were paralyzed.

At this point in our journey, the Israelite's had not been given the Law of Moses. The Lord had given them very few commands to obey. The commands He gave were not to leave any manna overnight, and on the sixth day, they were to collect and bake double the amount so they could rest on the sabbath. Food and water had such control of them, they couldn't even obey those two simple commands.

> *And Moses said, Let no man leave of it till the morning. Notwithstanding they hearkened not unto Moses; but some of them left of it till the morning, and it bred worms and stank: and Moses was wroth with them. (Exodus 16:19-20, KJV)*

> *And it came to pass, that there went out some of the people on the seventh day for to gather, and they found none. And the Lord said unto Moses, How long refuse ye to keep my commandments and my laws? (Exodus 16:27-28, KJV)*

The physical substances had so much control over the people that, even while knowing there would be fresh manna in the morning, they still had to take it upon themselves to ensure there would be manna by leaving some on the ground. This led to fear and worry, which led to disobedience, which led to the grumbling. We do the exact same thing.

As this chapter is ending think of the different ways we worry about food. Call it what it is, fear and worry. With the majority of us, our diets are defined by fear. List the reasons why your diet consists of what it does. If you are completely honest, then it will be recognizable that it is out of worry which is fear. If I eat this, then I'll gain weight. If I eat this amount, I'll stay thin. This food will clog my arteries, that food won't. See the disclaimer. I'm not trying to change your diet. But the first step in walking in divine health is just to recognize what the difference is between fear and faith.

4: The Law of Moses, Our First Instructor

Alright! Now is the time to take a coffee break. I'm waiting for my new coffee roaster to come today and am very excited about it. I'm running very low on roasted coffee beans for a reason, so I can try the roaster out right away. While we're sipping on our coffee, take that time to contemplate on the first three chapters. I want your spirit fully saturated with those points.

Up to this point in our journey, God hadn't placed the health of the children of Israel on food or water. The children of Israel did, not Moses or God. We've limited our discussion so far with Israel primarily to before the Law of Moses was enacted. A final point is from Egypt to Sinai when we can see there was no feeble among the children of Israel.

> *He brought them forth also with silver and gold: and there was not one feeble person among their tribes. (Psalm*

105:37, KJV)

All of the people were supernaturally healthy up to this point. There were no diseases attributed to food or anything else. Their health also was not attributed to food in any manner shape or form. With the institution of the Law of Moses, this all changed.

The whole book of Leviticus is about all the regulations which governed the animal sacrifices. All of these offerings had to be administered by the priests and had to be conducted in the temple. The first seven chapters of Leviticus covers all of the offerings. There are many, but essentially, there are five major categories. Below is a simple explanation. It is not essential to know, although it will be beneficial to have a little knowledge of it.

Burnt Offerings~ This offering was the most conducted and was to show submission to God's Will. None of this type of sacrifice was eaten.

Peace Offering~ This offering was a show of thanksgiving and gratitude towards God for his mercies. There was a portion of it burnt, a portion given to the priest to eat, and another portion eaten by the one offering the sacrifice.

Sin Offering~ This type of offering was an atonement for unintentional sin and eaten by the priest.

Guilt Offering~ This offering was to atone for stealing from the altar when it is unsure whether there has been a sin committed. This offering was eaten by the priest.

Food and Drink Offerings~ These were the offerings that represented giving the fruits of man's labor to God. A portion was burned, and a portion given to the priest.

> *And every oblation of thy meat offering shalt thou season with salt; neither shalt thou suffer the salt of the covenant of thy God to be lacking from thy meat offering: with all thine offerings thou shalt offer salt. (Leviticus 2:13, KJV)*

> *Ye are the salt of the earth: but if the salt have lost his savour, wherewith shall it be salted? It is thenceforth good for nothing, but to be cast out, and to be trodden under foot of men. (Matthew 5:13, KJV)*

Jesus called us the salt of the Earth. Salt was used on offerings to add flavor to meat. No sacrifice was to be given unless it was salted first. There is much significance to this that is lost on us, but the Jews understood it well. The whole reason that in the Old Covenant food played such an important role was to show spiritual truths.

In the New Covenant, the physical realities are included. This is the whole reason that God first declared to Noah that all things were given unto our hand long before the nation of Israel was set apart through Abraham and his sons. It set the stage for God to show us the spiritual truths through Israel and lead us into understanding the significance of Christ. Once revealed and fulfilled by Christ, then God's original purpose is restored. When it comes to food, his intent is shown by His words to Noah. When it comes to faith, it is shown by Abraham before the nation of Israel is born. Thus, God is showing us that His will is for all men to come to Him through Christ.

There is so much importance and meaning that is lost in all the offerings including the last supper. The end result is that, at the last supper, Jesus was pointing to himself as being the fulfillment of all of the Laws of Moses. Even more than that, He was also pointing to the end of food as being the primary sustenance of all life. In His representation of His body and blood, He re-directs us from meat (the animal sacrifices) to the bread (his body) as the sacrifice. This in turn, points to the manna sent down from heaven while the children of Israel were in their Exodus. So, Jesus is the manna sent from heaven and we are no longer subject to the effects of physical food. A bold statement, I know, as all of our earthly experiences point to the exact opposite (see the disclaimer once again).

We are going to still cover the Old Covenant. However, now, we're going to look at Jesus' views. Remember, Jesus was born under the Law of Moses and adhered to it perfectly. He fulfilled it while still showing us how the Father views food. He broke none of the dietary restrictions because He was sent to fulfill the Laws. Yet, there is much Jesus stated about food.

After Jesus fulfilled the Law of Moses and then was Resurrected, He sent us Paul to clarify what to believe about food as children of God. Keep this in mind as you read the rest of this chapter.

And when the tempter came to him, he said, If thou be the

Son of God, command that theses stones be made bread.
(Matthew 4:3, KJV)

The very first thing after Jesus had fasted 40 days, the devil tempted Him with food! Jesus is the second Adam. The first Adam had failed this temptation. This was the beginning of His earthly ministry and the first thing used to tempt Him was food. There is much significance in this. His answer should be our answer. Remember this book isn't about not eating. It is about putting things in their proper place.

> *But he answered and said, It is written, Man shall not*
> *live by bread alone, but by every word that proceedeth out*
> *of the mouth of God. (Matthew 4:4, KJV)*

Let us proceed as we take a sip of coffee. You see? I am about enjoying things that the Loving Father has given us!

> *No man can serve two masters: for either he will hate the*
> *one, and love the other; or else he will hold to the one, and*
> *despise the other. Ye cannot serve God and mammon.*
> *(Matthew 6:24, KJV)*

Most people believe and teach that this is in reference to money, it goes much deeper than that. He actually explains exactly what he means in the following scripture. Pay attention to the word *therefore* which directs us back to the word mammon.

> *Therefore I say unto you, Take no thought for your **life**,*
> *what ye shall **eat**, or what ye shall **drink**; nor yet for*
> *your **body**, what ye shall put on. Is not the life more than*
> ***meat**, and the **body** than raiment? (Matthew 6:25,*

KJV)

Mammon therefore is better defined as what physical things mankind looks upon as being precious and definitely includes food. In fact, Jesus doesn't even reference money in this whole expose'.

> *Behold the fowls of the air: for they sow not, neither do they reap, nor gather into barns; yet your heavenly Father feedeth them. Are ye not much better than they? (Matthew 6:26, KJV)*

Ouch! That has got to stop and make us think. A quick reminder: Jesus isn't referring to food being evil. Rather, it is our perspective on food that is. He doesn't stop there, Jesus keeps going.

> *Therefore take no thought, saying, What shall we eat? or, What shall we drink? or, Wherewithal shall we be clothed? (Matthew 6:31, KJV)*

Jesus didn't really mean those things, did He? I wonder if counting calories, planning what foods will keep us healthy, which foods are gluten free, sugar free, how many carbs to eat, etc., would qualify as giving heed to food? He still isn't stopping there. Keep in mind, I just really want you to ponder these verses. I know what we see as normal and those are the very things we need to question. The ways of a man seem right to him. That's paraphrased.

> *(For after all these things do the Gentiles seek:) for your heavenly Father knoweth that ye have need of all these things. But seek ye first the kingdom of God, and his righteousness; and all these things shall be added unto you. (Matthew 6:32-33, KJV)*

The Gentiles were all the people who were without God. They constantly worried about where their next meal was coming from. Jesus was talking to people that had the (testimony) of the manna from heaven in a jar! Seek God's kingdom first, and all these things shall be miraculously given to you. That would be called *adlibbing* just a bit. Didn't Jesus miraculously feed thousands and isn't He the embodiment of God's kingdom? I state that because it isn't an exaggeration.

> *So don't worry about tomorrow, for tomorrow will bring its own worries. Today's trouble is enough for today. (Matthew 6:34, NLT)*

I'm pretty sure when Jesus says we shouldn't worry, then we shouldn't worry. The trouble is deeper than just the typical trouble, but the same as sinning due to lack of faith in God when taken in context. Jesus is talking about anything that is contrary to faith in God as being evil. Seriously, as you read, ask Holy Spirit to speak to your heart as to whether I'm overreaching or speaking truth.

> *And he called the multitude, and said unto them, Hear, and understand: Not that which goeth into the mouth defileth a man; but that which cometh out of the mouth this defileth a man....And Jesus said, Are ye also yet without understanding? Do not ye yet understand, that whatsoever entereth in at the mouth goeth into the belly and is cast out into the draught? But those things which proceed out of the mouth come forth from the heart; and they defile the man. For out of the heart proceed evil thoughts, murders, adulteries, fornications, thefts, false witness, blasphemies: These are the things which defile a*

*man: but to eat with unwashen hands defileth not a man.
(Matthew 15:10-11, 16-20, KJV)*

Many of us just tumble over this and don't realize the significance of
it. Before I shock you, let's correct many wrong teachings on this
verse.

Many preachers teach that Jesus was declaring all food to be clean at
this point. That just isn't true. Jesus was born under the Law to fulfill
it. The *ritually* clean and unclean foods still existed, so that isn't what
he is saying at this point in time. He could not contradict the Law of
Moses that he was sent to fulfill. Here's a reminder, before the
crucifixion Jesus wasn't sent to everyone, but just to the children of
Israel:

> *But he answered and said, I am not sent but unto the lost
> sheep of the house of Israel (Matthew 15:24, KJV).*

He could and did contradict the traditions of men that the pharisees
had added to the Laws of Moses such as the ceremonial washing of
the hands, which in this day and age of hand sanitizer, is abhorrent to
us. He was saying that not washing of the hands isn't what affects the
body, but what comes out of the mouth. It isn't germs that will cause
us to be sick, but the condition of our heart and what we speak.

Let me state for the record, I do wash my hands. That's just the right
thing to do. Not out of fear of getting some germ. I have no fear of
that. It is out of respect for others. Nevertheless, the point is, when
we are truly walking in the spirit, what we put into our mouths
should not affect us. Rather, it should be neutral. It is neither good

nor bad. After Jesus fulfills the Law as I will continue to show you, there is no longer the ritually clean or unclean. Things revert back to God's decree to Noah that all things are given unto us.

> *Labour not for the meat which perisheth, but for that meat which endureth unto everlasting life, which the Son of man shall give unto you: for him hath God the Father sealed. (John 6:27, KJV)*

Hold your breath my friends. Here comes the kicker!

> *Our fathers did eat manna in the desert; as it is written, He gave them bread from heaven to eat. (John 6:31, KJV)*

This statement isn't from Jesus. It's from those listening to him and probably spoken by the pharisees. Check out the response from Jesus:

> *Then Jesus said unto them, Verily, verily, I say unto you, Moses* **gave you not** *that bread from heaven; but my Father giveth you the true bread from heaven. For the bread of God is he which cometh down from heaven, and giveth life unto the world. (John 6:32-33, KJV)*

> *And Jesus said unto them, I am the bread of life: he that cometh to me shall never hunger; and he that believeth on me shall never thirst. (John 6:35, KJV)*

We want to dismiss this and think that Jesus was only talking about this in its spiritual connotation. We rationalize and dilute it down to mean that when we get to heaven, there will be no need for food. Yet, Christ brought heaven to earth! We put off many blessings and truths by not recognizing the spiritual truth is active now, and when we believe, it overcomes what we see as truth in the physical world. The greater the truth is, the more spiritual the truth even in the physical world. Regardless of what our experience dictates, the spiritual truth is the one that overcomes the physical boundaries of this world. Mankind is only in its infancy when it comes to truly learning what is available today through putting these spiritual truths into practice. So, the key is to push the envelope, push the physical boundaries, and truly start believing that *nothing is impossible for those that believe.*

Nowhere, even in proverbs, is healing or health attributed to what we put into our mouths. In the many, many scriptures that talk about long life and health, not one of them name food. Death and life are in what you eat? Nope. That isn't the verse at all. Here's just one example of many that are in the book of proverbs.

> *A man's belly shall be satisfied with the fruit of his mouth; and with the increase of his lips shall he be filled. Death and life are in the power of the tongue: and they that love it shall eat the fruit thereof. (Proverbs 18:20-21, KJV)*

Nowhere in his earthly ministry did Jesus say that food or what goes in the mouth will give eternal life except when referencing himself. Nor did he ever tell a person to go eat this or that type of food to be healed. In fact, he never used food in any of the individual healings that are recounted in scriptures. He never ever referenced food as a healer, yet we do. He used bread at the last supper, but that was in reference to himself not to the physical substance. The physical substance bread was to be used as a reminder that he is the bread of life.

> *The Jews then murmured at him, because he said, I am the bread which came down from heaven. (John 6:41, KJV)*

"But Tony, you're wrong. Paul told Timothy to drink wine because of his stomach ailments." Uh oh! Hmm, really? Look above. Just as Jesus is referencing Himself, not the physical substance of bread, so Paul is doing the same thing. Paul is pointing Timothy right to Jesus and the New Covenant. Wine would've brought Timothy to remember the Last Supper. Another point is that Holy Spirit is represented by wine. He wasn't telling Timothy to use wine for "a cure" or for medicinal value. Instead, he is telling him to remember Christ while eating and drinking. The first letter to Timothy was when he (Timothy) was young in the faith. Paul is reminding him and instructing him. Compare First Timothy to Second Timothy which was written six years later. Second Timothy is written to a mature believer and there is no further mentioning of Timothy's stomach or often infirmities.

Jesus and only Jesus is our bread of Life and we should give credit to none other than him for our health and wellbeing. With that stated, we are going to switch gears in the next chapter. I'm going to show how scriptures confirm the command of God to Noah that all foods are given to us for consumption. In the New Covenant, all things are become clean and the ritual (ceremonial) clean and unclean descriptions for food are no longer relevant. And you thought that I am against food! I'm not.

5: What God Has Declared to Be Clean

Aha! It looks like we've made it to chapter five. You've stuck with me this far. Oops! I am out of coffee and the pot is empty. While my coffee is brewing, allow me to back up for a minute to discuss the Daniel fast.

There are those that say the Daniel's fast is God's diet and think it is God showing us the divine diet. Sorry, that just isn't correct. Daniel was under the Old Covenant Laws which made it unlawful to eat food sacrificed to idols. In Babylonian culture, it was believed that one had to eat meat in order to be healthy. What Daniels fast proves is that man's wisdom isn't true when it comes to servants of God Almighty. He sustained Daniel and his companions in spite of human wisdom saying otherwise. That is what the Daniel fast shows us, not what food in the New Covenant is considered to be the divine diet. My testimony goes even farther.

My going six months without food or drink because of a paralyzed stomach shows that God will sustain humans without any food if needed! He is no respecter of persons. Therefore, it isn't that I'm just some kinda special person. God will do that for anyone. Coffee's done! So, let's move it along to the book of Acts.

Here's where I start disputing the bad teachings that try to bring us under the Law of Moses dietary restrictions (Like I haven't been already doing that). Do you ever wonder why a diet is so hard to follow if you are on a strict medical diet or trying to lose weight? It's because we, doctors, and even preachers innocently enough put ourselves under the Law of sin which was embedded by the enemy into the Law of Moses. This was the tactic the serpent used in the garden of Eden.

> *For that which I do I allow not: for what I would, that do I not; but what I hate, that do I. If then I do that which I would not, I consent unto the law that it is good. Now then it is no more I that do it, but sin that dwelleth in me. For I know that in me (that is, in my flesh,) dwelleth no good thing: for to will is present with me; but how to perform that which is good I find not. For the good that I would I do not: but the evil which I would not, that I do. Now if I do that I would not, it is no more I that do it, but sin that dwelleth in me. I find then a law, that, when I would do good, evil is present with me. For I delight in the law of God after the inward man: But I see another law in my members, warring against the law of my mind, and bringing me into captivity to the law of sin which is in my members. (Romans 7:15-23, KJV)*

Simply put, when we're told *not* to do something (or if we ourselves

45

are determined not to do something), we do it. If we're not walking in the spirit, if we're focused on the physical senses, then we are captive to the law of sin. Try telling an alcoholic not to drink. His focus is then on not drinking which will lead him straight to the nearest bar or liquor store. We can hate our actions, be sincere in our declaration not to do it, and yet we end up doing that which we hate. The solution will come later on in the book when I'm laying out the solution on overcoming the physical senses.

Let's get back to the book of Acts. There are two accounts written that we're gonna look at in the book of Acts. Peter's vision is the first:

> *And he became very hungry, and would have eaten: but while they made ready, he fell into a trance, and saw heaven opened, and a certain vessel descending unto him, as it had been a great sheet knit at the four corners, and let down to the earth: Wherein were all manner of four footed beasts of the earth and wild beasts, and creeping things, and fowls of the air. And there came a voice to him, Rise, Peter; kill, and eat. But Peter said, Not so, Lord; for I have never eaten anything that is common or unclean. And the voice spake unto him again the second time, What God hath cleansed, that call not thou common. This was done thrice: and the vessel was received up again into heaven. (Acts 10:10-16, KJV)*

There is absolutely no doubt that the reason for this vision was that the gospel of Christ was to be preached to the gentiles as well.

> *Then Peter opened his mouth, and said, Of a truth I perceive that God is no respecter of persons: But in every nation he that feareth him, and worketh righteousness, is accepted with him. The word which God sent unto the*

children of Israel, preaching peace by Jesus Christ: (he is
Lord of all:) (Acts 10:34-36, KJV)

The debate comes about by leaders dismissing that this vision also applied to physical food. The argument is that Peter had not changed his diet in ten years, so the Jewish diet should remain intact. Let's look at this for a minute.

First of all, why would Peter change his diet? He had eaten that way his whole life. It had become his food of preference. Since the source of life is the Bread of Life, Jesus, why would Peter's diet need to change? Food isn't the issue with God. When a person say from Cuba comes and settles in the U.S., doesn't their preference in food remain the same? Yes, they will try other foods, but on the whole, their favorite food is what they're familiar with.

I grew up eating Italian food. My favorite food remains Italian. So, the argument that Peter hadn't eaten any unclean food does not hold any water whatsoever. In fact, it is the reason why God used the animals and told Peter to eat. Nations and countries are defined by what they eat. A person from Spain eats Spanish food, a person from Mexico eats Mexican, so on and so forth. Therefore, this vision was also telling Peter that all persons and their food was acceptable to Him. Nowhere in the book of Acts do any of the Apostles giving a witness of Jesus Christ tell a person that in order to become a believer, you must change your diet.

The spiritual truth is also the physical truth whether we believe that or not. God's truth is the truth. The Loving Father is not double-minded nor is he a hypocrite. Therefore, His sending a vision involving all animals being clean to eat means exactly that.

God doesn't use a lie to emphasize a greater truth. The ritualistic clean and unclean foods were just that, a ritual for the Jews so that they could understand the deeper spiritual meaning that all people who believe in Christ are His when the appointed time would come. Peter's vision is showing him that this was the appointed time and that all people including their food are acceptable to Him.

Indeed, the Judaizers tried to do the same thing with circumcision. Jesus had stated that it isn't the physical circumcision that mattered, but the circumcision of the heart. Paul further reinforces the views on circumcision and food. Food is no different. The type of food you eat has no bearing upon whether one is a true believer or not, nor should it be the controller of whether we are healthy or not. Rather, when we believe that He is the giver and Bread of Life, it is His Holy Spirit who will sustain us, not our diet.

Circumcision and the Jewish food laws were one in the same. Both were an indicator that they were a nation separated unto God for a period of time. Both circumcision and the kosher diet went hand in hand, separating the nation of Israel from other nations. With His Sacrifice, Jesus broke down that wall of separation. The Law of Moses was then fulfilled.

> *For he is our peace, who hath made both one, and hath*
> *broken down the middle wall of partition between us;*
> *Having abolished in his flesh the enmity, even the law of*

commandments contained in ordinances; for to make in himself of twain one new man, so making peace; And that he might reconcile both unto God in one body by the cross having slain the enmity thereby: (Ephesians 2:14-16, KJV)

The middle wall of separation was the ordinances. The ordinances included the ritually clean and unclean food restrictions. In becoming our peace, He was making one *new man*. You see that, right?

There is neither Jew nor Greek, there is neither bond nor free, there is neither male nor female: for ye are all one in Christ Jesus. (Galation 3:28, KJV)

This means that the food ordinances are lifted. It also means that now, all foods are acceptable to the Father. There is no one diet that is any better than another. There is no one diet that God views as *the one* that will keep you healthy because He's personally blessed it. Scratch that. There is one diet and He's called the Bread of Life, Christ Jesus!

Now we're switching gears to a chapter that is always neglected when it comes to proponents of a so-called Divine Diet.

But there rose up a certain of the sect of the Pharisees which believed, saying, That it was needful to circumcise them, and to **command them to keep the law of Moses.** *(Acts 15:5, KJV)*

This is my sarcastic moment: *Hello!* Go to the book of Leviticus please. Leviticus and Deuteronomy are the books of the Law of Moses. Both these books are all about the ritually clean and unclean foods, especially Leviticus which is all about the offerings and sacrifices. Let us see what Peter, who received the vision about all the creatures of the earth being clean. has to say about that.

> *And when there had been much disputing, Peter rose up, and said unto them, Men and brethren, ye know how that a good while ago God made choice among us, that the Gentiles by my mouth should hear the word of the gospel, and believe. And put no difference between us and them, purifying their hearts by faith. (Acts 15:7, 9, KJV)*

Wait for the zinger, here it comes!

> *Now therefore why tempt ye God, to put a yoke upon the neck of the disciples, which neither our fathers nor we were able to bear? (Acts 15:10, KJV)*

Peter who himself hadn't eaten any unclean creature is declaring that Gentiles are not subject to the ordinances of the Law of Moses, which does consist of the book of Leviticus in which all the food laws and restrictions are contained. In fact, he is declaring that they are tempting God by even suggesting it. Let's see what James has to say:

> *Wherefore my sentence is, that we trouble not them, which from among the Gentiles are turned to God; But that we write unto them, that they abstain from pollutions of idols, and from fornication, and from things strangled, and from blood. (Acts 15:19-20, KJV)*

Yet, guess what? There is something very much missing from James sentence. If there is no change in diet, then why doesn't James include not eating fat? My dear friends, if the sentence of not eating blood stands, then why isn't the ordinance of not eating fat in the declaration made by James? It's specifically in the book of Leviticus, so don't try to say James absentmindedly left it out.

> *It shall be a perpetual statute for your generations throughout all your dwellings, that ye eat neither fat nor blood. (Leviticus 3:17, KJV)*

Fat is missing somewhere else as well.

> *But the flesh with the life thereof, which is the blood thereof, shall ye not eat. (Genesis 9:4, KJV).*

Once again, it takes us right back to where God declares to Noah all creatures are given to us, not to the Law of Moses and the Jewish restrictions, just in case you're still trying to rationalize this. Letters were written to the gentile churches and this is what was written:

> *Forasmuch as we have heard, that certain which went out from us have troubled you with words, subverting your souls, saying, Ye must be circumcised, **and keep the law: to whom we gave no such commandment.** (Acts 15:24, KJV)*

> *That ye abstain from meats offered to idols, and from blood, and from things strangled, and from fornication: from which if ye keep yourselves, ye shall do well. Fare ye well. (Acts 15:29, KJV)*

This is from James, the apostles, and the elders in Jerusalem that made this ruling. This was not a decision that Paul alone made. As stated, the book of Leviticus that contains the ordinances of the Law

h clearly, the Holy Spirit through James and the

were not part of the New Covenant. Many people

..postles still following the Law of Moses. In fact, they

uid. In order that they be able to reach the Jews, they had to continue

in the Law of Moses including the animal sacrifices.

> *Even though I am a free man with no master, I have become a slave to all people to bring many to Christ. When I was with the Jews, I lived like a Jew to bring the Jews to Christ. When I was with those who follow the Jewish law, I too lived under that law. Even though I am not subject to the law, I did this so I could bring to Christ those who are under the law. When I am with the Gentiles who do not follow the Jewish law, I too live apart from that law so I can bring them to Christ…. (1 Corinthians 9:19-21, NLT)*

Those who lived in Jerusalem, in fact, had to do the same thing to reach the Jews who still followed the Law of Moses. The Apostles were not in fact following the Law of Moses as an example for us today, but out of necessity for the sake of the gospel

> *Do therefore this that we say to thee: We have four men which have a vow on them: Them take, and purify thyself with them, and be at charges with them, that they may shave their heads: and all may know that those things, whereof they were informed concerning thee, are nothing; but that thou thyself also walkest orderly, and keepest the law. As touching the Gentiles which believe, we have written and concluded that* **they observe no such thing,** *save only that they keep themselves from things offered to idols, and from blood, and from strangled, and from fornication. Then Paul took the men, and the next*

day purifying himself with them entered into the temple, to signify the accomplishment of the days of purification, until that an offering should be offered for every one of them. (Acts 21: 23-26, KJV)

Now after many years I came to bring alms to my nation, and offerings. (Acts 24:17, KJV)

Do you not yet see? The arguments that are used to support that the dietary restrictions are still intact are not true. Paul did animal offerings in spite of the fact they were no longer needed, out of necessity. This is also why Paul was so harsh on the Gentile churches that were being led into Judaism. Notice though in the scripture above, the statement *after many years*. He did those things not to follow or enforce Jewish customs, but for the cause of Christ.

Oh, foolish Galatians! Who has cast an evil spell on you? For the meaning of Jesus Christ's death was made as clear to you as if you had seen a picture of his death on the cross. Let me ask you this one question: Did you receive the Holy Spirit by obeying the law of Moses? Of course not! You received the Spirit because you believed the message you heard about Christ. How foolish can you be? After starting your new lives in the Spirit, why are now trying to become perfect by your own human effort. Have you experienced so much for nothing? Surely it was not in vain, was it? (Galatians 3:1-3, NLT)

When teachers point to Peter, Paul, John, and James and say they followed the Jewish customs. Now you are informed as to the reasons why. A little in-depth study and listening to the Holy Spirit will show you that this is all true. With this knowledge we are now ready to plunge into the actual New Covenant teachings about how we should view food.

6: The Corruption of Judaizers and Gnostics

Are you ready? We are now going to start dealing with food and what we put into our mouths on a more spiritual level as the children of God. We've still got a lot more busting walls down to do, but we are now onto the spiritual truths.

These previous chapters were quite needed because there is much confusion when it comes to food. The confusion is caused by the human experience and the many misperceptions of well-meaning leaders in the body of Christ. The Truth is what sets us free. If we aren't set free, then we either haven't heard the truth or we haven't accepted the truth. Here's another bit of truth: I love coffee! Let's sit down and have us a good hot mug..

One of the most troubling teachings I've heard, is about Colossians 2:16.

So don't let anyone condemn you for what you eat or drink,
or for not celebrating certain holy days or new moon
ceremonies or Sabbaths. (Colossians 2:16, NLT)

This troubling teaching says that the Colossians were being influenced by Gnostics and that he was confirming that gentile believers should be celebrating the Jewish feasts, customs, and observances. In other words, that the Law of Moses still applied. I've already covered that in the previous chapter with the command of James that is in Acts 15:20. Now, we're going to break it down even farther in context to totally disprove this.

In this letter, Paul was not advocating a return to the Law of Moses or the definition of clean and unclean animals.

I wanted you to know how much I have agonized for you
and for the church at Laodicea, and for many other believers
who have never met me personally. (Colossians 2:1, NLT)

Paul specifically references the church of Laodicea and many other believers. According to my research, the problem with this church wasn't the influence of Gnostics. Paul was agonizing over a matter concerning both churches. The Colossians were being influenced by the Gnostics while the Laodiceans by the Judaizers. One thing that Gnostics were known for was considering all physical comforts as being evil. They would also spiritualize everything including worshipping of angels and living in extreme denial of self. There were two camps of bad teachings that came from the converted Jews: one, the strict enforcement of the Law of Moses, the Judaizers; the other, Gnosticism.

Paul addresses both of these false beliefs throughout Colossians, and more specifically, in the second chapter. He leads all believers right back to Christ being the head of the church, nullifying both false teachings. With that being the case, when Paul wrote, "Let no one condemn you by what you eat or drink or the holy days, etc., he was warning them about both sides of the fence as is supported in many other scriptures when Paul talks about food. We'll get to those scriptures in the next chapter. Meanwhile, let's talk about how Paul is referencing both false camps.

> ....I want them to have complete confidence that they understand God's mysterious plan, which is Christ himself. In him lie hidden all the treasure of wisdom and knowledge. I am telling you this **so no one** will deceive you with well-crafted arguments. (Colossians 2:2-4, NLT)

The gentile believers were getting hit from both sides of the extreme which we do today as well. Many gnostic beliefs are spread within the body of Christ as well as the Pharisaical mindset. The early believers had this same condition. Paul is writing so they are warned of both factions.

> Beware lest any man spoil you through philosophy and vain deceit, after the tradition of men, after the rudiments of the world, and not after Christ. (Colossians 2:8, KJV)

Paul is referring to both sides because it actually is the same coin. Jesus makes it clear in the following scripture.

> For John came neither eating nor drinking, and they say, He hath a devil. The Son of man came eating and drinking, and

*they say, Behold a man gluttonous, and a winebibber, a
friend of publicans and sinners. But wisdom is justified of
her children.(Matthew 11:18-19, KJV)*

In this passage Jesus is pointing to both factions of the Pharisees, those
who had a Gnostic mindset and those who had a stricter, rigid mindset.
In Colossians, we are now to where Paul is pointing the finger directly
at the Judaizers.

In whom also ye are circumcised with the **circumcision
made without hands,** *in putting off the body of the sins
of the flesh by the circumcision of Christ: (Colossians 2:11,
KJV)*

*He canceled the record of the charges against us and took it
away, by nailing it to the cross. In this way, he disarmed the
spiritual rulers and authorities. He shamed them publicly by
his victory over them on the cross. So don't let* **anyone**
*condemn you for what you eat or drink, or for not celebrating
certain holy days or new moon ceremonies or Sabbaths. For
these rules are only shadows of the reality yet to come.* **And
Christ himself is that reality.** *(Colossians 2:14-17,
NLT)*

Stop right there. All of that is directed to the Judaizers who wanted
everyone to continue in the ways of the Law of Moses. By spiritual
rulers and authorities, Paul means both the human authorities and the
office of Satan as well. Many will think that he was talking only about
the office of Satan, but he is referencing the human spiritual leaders as
well, the high priests of the Jews and the pharisees who Jesus had
publicly shamed. For these rules, which are the ordinances written in
the Law of Moses, are only shadows of the reality yet to come. Many

people think (because the way it is translated) that we are still waiting for that reality. We aren't, as Paul states, but Christ himself is that reality. Up to this point, Paul is talking about the Judaizers who were trying to turn everyone including the Gentiles back to the Law of Moses. In the very next verse, Paul shifts the conversation to the Gnostics.

> **Don't let anyone condemn you** *by insisting on pious self-denial or the worship of angels, saying they have had visions about these things. Their sinful minds have made them proud, and they are not connected to Christ, the head of the body. For he holds the whole body together with its joints and ligaments, and it grows as God nourishes it. (Colossians 2:18-19, NLT)*

"Don't let anyone condemn you" means that Paul is redirecting what he's talking about. He changed the subject from the gnostic teachings of pious self-denial, that food is evil, and angels were to be worshiped, to the truth of freedom in Christ. Not only did these self-professed Christians teach those things, but they also taught that Christ had not come in the flesh, rather only in the spiritual sense. This is the reason that Paul states those who believe such things are not connected to Christ.

Then from verse twenty on, he ties both false teachings together. The common thread to both is that they are wisdom of men: self-sufficiency instead of trust in God, and false worship of creations rather than creator. Both the teachings have to do with physical substances which do not lead to Christ. In other words, the same laws that state that what we eat or touch affects whether we are clean or unclean (holy or unholy).

> *You have died with Christ, and he has set you free from the*
> *spiritual powers of this world. So why do you keep on*
> *following the rules of the world, such as, "Don't handle!*
> *Don't taste! Don't touch!"? Such rules are mere human*
> *teachings about things that deteriorate as we use them. These*
> *rules may seem wise because they require strong devotion,*
> *pious self-denial, and severe bodily discipline. But they*
> *provide no help in conquering a person's evil desires.*
> *(Colossians 2:20-23, NLT)*

Do you see how Paul is literally condemning both of these sects? Both had their start in Judaism carried into Christianity by those falsely professing to be converted. And once again, both of these beliefs are easily stomped by James declaration in Acts 15.

> *Forasmuch as we have heard, that certain which went out*
> *from us have troubled you with words, subverting your souls,*
> *saying, Ye must be circumcised, **and keep the law: to***
> ***whom we gave no such commandment:** (Acts*
> *15:24, KJV)*

> *Wherefore my sentence is, that we trouble not them, which*
> *from among the Gentiles are turned to God; But that we*
> *write unto them, that they abstain from pollutions of idols,*
> *and from fornication, and from things strangled, and from*
> *blood. (Acts 15:19-20, KJV)*

Are you starting to see that food or anything we put into our mouths should be viewed as neutral? It is neither good nor evil and is subject to only where we place it. In most cases, the majority of Believers put these things on a pedestal, allowing them the power to control their lives. Here's another explosive thought. Scripture says:

A man's belly shall be satisfied with the fruit of his mouth; and with the increase of his lips shall he be filled. Death and life are in the power of the tongue: and they that love it shall eat the fruit thereof. (Proverbs 18: 20-21, KJV)

Here's what we say:

A man's belly shall be satisfied by what we put into our mouths; and with the increased eating of food, we shall become fat. Death and life are in the power of our diet: and they that eat properly shall live a long life. Those that do not eat properly shall surely die soon (Proverbs of Human Wisdom, Tony Style).

This is how most of us live! Think about it. That is exactly what we say by our words and actions. Dearest sisters and brothers in Christ, how many times have you thought or said. "I shouldn't eat this or I will get fat!" By speaking that and believing it, we are indeed causing it to happen. Did that catch your attention?

I've spent a whole chapter on Chapter 2 of Colossians because it is so mistaught and misunderstood. I do want to clarify a few things. Just to make sure that it is absolutely clear, I am not against celebrating the Jewish feasts when done with a correct belief of the heart. The feasts were all pointing to Christ. They were all fulfilled with Christ's coming and His Resurrection. There is possibly one exception, depending on your viewpoint, The Feast of the Trumpets which I'm not going into. With the possible exception of that one feast, all others have been fulfilled by Christ.

So, if you are celebrating the feasts in a spirit of thanksgiving that these feasts are completed, then that is very acceptable to the Lord. Whether we celebrate the feasts or not, that isn't the issue. Do all things to God's Glory. In Christ, the Sabbath has been fulfilled. But if we celebrate the Sabbath knowing that it is fulfilled in Him, it is acceptable to the Father. Whether we adhere to the Sabbath or whether we don't, it is acceptable when either celebrated or not celebrated with the right heart. The same holds true for food. Still not convinced? Then read Romans 14:5-7 which says exactly what I just stated.

7: Food is Good, Our Perception of It Isn't

This is the last chapter that focuses on proving that all things created by God for consumption are good. We should enjoy what The Father has given us. There are so many scriptures proving this statement in the New Testament, that really, I could just make a whole chapter of them with no commentary.

For instance, all of Romans 14 covers this very specifically. I could put the whole chapter here and prove that what I'm saying is true. It is often taught that there need be at least two scriptural references to prove a teaching. That being the case, I've already gone beyond that. But because as a people we are stubborn and do not easily change our thoughts or beliefs, which is not a bad thing, I will continue to show that under the New Covenant, there are no dietary restrictions. Then we'll get to the solution portion of this book, and part of the solution is believing the Truth. It's a cold day outside, so I really do appreciate my coffee!

As I've already pointed out, converted Jews were trying to bring gentile believers under the Law of Moses. They were judging these believers on the basis of what they ate. This was causing much strife in the body of Christ along with much confusion. In Romans 14, Paul is telling them to follow their conscience, but not put a stumbling block onto others.

Just because I know it'll come up, as is stated at the beginning of this book, I don't care what you eat or don't eat, what diet you're on or not on. It makes no difference to me. So, I am not judging you by what you eat. My only desire is for all of us to grow more mature spiritually and have a long life living in God's Kingdom now, to continue to spread His kingdom throughout this planet, and that we may all become unified unto Our Lord Christ Jesus.

> *Him that is weak in the faith receive ye, but not to doubtful disputations. For one believeth that he may eat all things: another, who is weak, eateth herbs. (Romans 14:1-2, KJV)*

Hey, I didn't say that. Paul did and it has nothing to do with meat offered to idols. Let's continue:

> *In the same way, some think one day is more holy than another day, while others think every day is alike.* **You should each be fully convinced** *that whichever day you choose is acceptable. Those who worship the Lord on a special day do it to honor him. Those who eat any kind of food do so to honor the Lord, since they give thanks to God before eating. And those who refuse to eat certain foods also*

want to please the Lord and give thanks to God. (Romans 14:5-6, NLT)

Note: I didn't post this at the end of the last chapter, because here it is! Here's the important part of this scripture: that each person be convinced that whichever way you believe, it is acceptable. Whether you worship the Lord on Saturday, Sunday, or everyday, or don't eat certain foods, be convinced in your own mind that it is acceptable to the Lord without judging what another believes. Be convinced of yourself for your own sake.

> *I know, and am persuaded by the Lord Jesus,* **that there is nothing unclean of itself***: but to him that esteemeth any thing unclean, to him it is unclean. (Romans 14:14, KJV)*

> *For meat destroy not the work of God.* **All things indeed are pure***; but it is evil for that man who eateth with offence. (Romans 14:20, KJV)*

There is no way that these scriptures can be misunderstood. There is an argument some use in trying to dismiss that Paul really does mean all foods. They will state that Paul isn't really saying that all animals are clean. He is only speaking of foods offered to idols. They are using that as an argument to say that the clean and unclean animal laws in Leviticus still stand. This argument is foolishness. Would you like to know why? We are talking about pagans that had no laws about clean and unclean foods. Both Romans and Greeks offered pigs to idols. There are even pagans who offered horses to idols. If Paul wasn't referencing all animals (or all things), he would have included a warning to avoid unclean foods in the marketplace.

> *Whatsoever is sold in the shambles, that eat, asking no questions for conscience sake: For the earth is the Lord's and the fulness thereof. (1 Corinthians 10:25, KJV)*

He is writing this knowing full well that unclean foods were sold in the marketplace. There is no warning from Paul about being careful with the food they choose. In fact, he is stating once again that everything is clean. People will argue, "Well, he wouldn't have to warn them because a pig would be obvious. They would just walk by it.

> *If any of them that believe not bid you to a feast, and ye be disposed to go; whatsoever is set before you, eat, asking no question for conscience sake. (1 Corinthians 10:27, KJV)*

Pigs would've been served at a feast, not to mention many other things considered "unclean" as well. Paul meant what he wrote and wrote what he meant. Do you see how those wishing to put restrictions on us have to go out of their way to manipulate the truth? They cannot come up with one scripture in the New Testament that states to keep the dietary restrictions of the Law of Moses. Not one! Meanwhile, I easily come up with many scriptures supporting my beliefs.

In writing this book, it is so clear that I could've just put chapter after chapter of nothing but scriptures supporting what I'm teaching. The opposing side cannot. They have to redefine what Paul is stating. They have to add to it and take away crucial scriptures in order to have any footing at all. There are also other scriptures that I've left out since there are so many scriptures validating my viewpoint. I was forced to pick and choose which to use or I would've just published most of the New Testament.

Because of this fact, many ministers will submit that all things are clean, but then they will state that The heavenly Father created us and knows which foods are good for our bodies and which aren't. They will state that the reason He put the food laws into effect was to show us what foods are healthy and what foods aren't healthy (the dietary restrictions are for our own good). They claim that the Old Covenant diet is the healthiest choice. Nothing could be farther from the truth.

In fact, secular studies have shown that health does not explain the restrictions of the Jewish diet. For example, camel and rabbit meat (unclean) are no less healthy than cow or goat meat. In fact, most Orthodox Jews cannot explain the reason for the restrictions.

I've already explained the reason for this. In the Old Covenant, He separated the Jews from the Gentiles to point the way to Jesus. Once the law was fulfilled by Jesus, He used the clean and unclean animals to show the Jews that all people are declared to be clean by faith In Christ. One such example is Peter's vision in Acts.

Many preachers still teach that if we don't take care of our bodies by watching what we put into our mouths, then it is sin. That is exactly opposite of what Paul is stating. In fact, these same preachers are disregarding what Paul is stating. They are causing other people to look down upon those who believe that they can eat anything. You walk by someone eating bacon and go to warn them. "Dear brother, your body is the temple of the Holy Spirit. You better not eat that bacon." "Oops, brother! Better not eat that candy! You're destroying the temple of God."

We don't realize this, but we are eating unto offense. Because a person puts one piece of candy into their mouths, no matter how much you rationalize this based off your experience, you just wrongly accused them of desecrating the temple of God! That my dear friends is a problem. "But Tony, gluttony is a sin, and that person was fat, so they are glutenous. Therefore, they are desecrating God's temple." Here's Paul's statement on that, which I'm paraphrasing: *mind your own business!* In fact, you should probably go back and read the disclaimer. I'm not advocating gluttony, but that is totally between them and God. Let's go ahead and cover that very well-known verse, and that since it's used in most pulpit's today wrongly, it is causing many to stumble and fall.

> *Know ye not that ye are the temple of God, and that the Spirit of God dwelleth in you? If any man defile the temple of God, him shall God destroy; for the temple of God is holy which temple ye are. (1 Corinthians 3:16, 17, KJV)*

> **For meat destroy not the work of God. All things indeed are pure;...** *(Romans 14:20, KJV)*

Now, go and read that scripture in context. It isn't even talking about food. It is talking about building upon the foundation that Christ has set, which wasn't set upon food. Got it? And the kingdom of God isn't about food or drink. Could that be made any more clear or do I really have to bring up everything I've taught to this point?

> *For the kingdom of God is not in meat and drink; but*
> *righteousness, and peace, and joy in the Holy Ghost.*
> *(Romans 14:17, KJV)*

Here is yet another scripture taken out of context, used to condemn others' eating habits.

> *What? Know ye not that your body is the temple of the Holy*
> *Ghost which is in you, which ye have of God, and ye are not*
> *your own? For ye are bought with a price: therefore glorify*
> *God in your body, and in your spirit, which are God's.(1*
> *Corinthians 6:19-20, KJV)*

In fact, this is so taken out of context that rarely is the real topic even mentioned. It is most often applied to what we put into our body, not to what Paul was talking about, which is fornication.

> *You say, "I am allowed to do anything"-but not everything*
> *is good for you. And even though "I am allowed to do*
> *anything," I must not become a slave to anything. You say,*
> *"Food was made for the stomach, and the stomach for food."*
> *(this is true, though someday God will do away with both of*
> *them.) But you can't say that our bodies were made for*
> *sexual immorality. They were made for the Lord, and the*
> *Lord cares about our bodies. And God will raise us from*
> *the dead by his power, just as he raised our Lord from the*
> *dead. Don't you realize that your bodies are actually parts of*
> *Christ? Should a man take his body, which is part of*
> *Christ, and join it to a prostitute? Never! (1 Corinthians*
> *6:12-15, NLT)*

> *Flee fornication. Every sin that a man doeth, is without the*
> *body; but he that committeth fornication sinneth against his*
> *own body. What? Know ye not that your body is the temple*
> *of the Holy Ghost which is in you, which ye have of God,*

and ye are not your own? For ye are bought with a price: therefore glorify God in your body, and in your spirit, which are God's. (1 Corinthians 6:18-20, KJV)

The whole reason Paul used food is because the Corinthians were comparing the belly being specifically made for food and using that as an excuse to commit sexual sin. They thought that since it is lawful to eat anything, therefore, it must be lawful to have intercourse with anyone. That was their thought process.

Paul agrees with this when it comes to food. However, when it came to sexual intercourse, there is a sharp rebuke. That is what this scripture is all about. Yet, we take it completely out of context so as to judge people by their eating habits.

With that said, I will state this in the same breath. Most of us are controlled by food, which we should not be. I wholeheartedly agree with that. But it is because we give it power in ways (until this book), that most don't recognize and regard as normal.

We give food power and control by thinking that it is the primary key to good health and a long life! Have you ever thought to yourself "I really would like more butter on my bread, but I don't need the cholesterol?" You just gave food control over your body. Or do you go out of your way to count calories? Hmmmmm? What is controlling you then?

The opposite is true as well. If we live to eat anything and everything, then we've given food control as well. If we use food as a means of comfort (instead of Our true comforter, Holy Spirit), we've just done the same thing. We have just given food, drink, or medicine power and control, therefore, it is the god of our lives.

> *As concerning therefore the eating of those things that are offered in sacrifice unto idols, we know that an idol is nothing in the world, and that there is none other God but one, For though there be that are called gods, whether in heaven or in earth, (as there be gods many, and lords many,) But to us there is but one God, the Father, of whom are all things and we in him; and one Lord Jesus Christ, by whom are all things, and we by him. Howbeit there is not in every man that knowledge: for some with conscience of the idol unto this hour eat it as a thing offered unto an idol; and their conscience being weak is defiled. But meat commendeth us not unto God: for neither, if we eat, are we the better; neither, if we eat not, are we the worse. (1 Corinthians 8:4-8, KJV)*

In other words, we don't win God's favor by what we eat. Whether we eat the food or not is of no consequence unless we eat it as if it's offered to a real god. It isn't our diet, that the Father is worried about. There is only one way to the Father and it's through belief in His Son, not by our diet. This lends even more weight to the fact that what is put into our mouth is neutral.

I'm so excited! We are almost to the point where I can get over, disproving the many scriptural misperceptions. We're almost to the point I can start offering solutions to our many struggles with food! In doing that, I'll be able to show how to overcome our reliance on the physical senses, in which case, your healing will manifest. In any book written by me, that is the end goal: to rely on Holy Spirit for all our needs. We've got one more scripture to cover, so let's get it on.

> *Now the Spirit speaketh expressly, that in the latter times some shall depart from the faith, giving heed to seducing spirits, and doctrines of devils; Speaking lies in hypocrisy; having their conscience seared with a hot iron; Forbidding to marry,* **commanding to abstain from meats** *(food), which God hath created to be received with thanksgiving of them which believe and know the truth.* **For every creature of God is good, and nothing to be refused, if it be received with thanksgiving: For it is sanctified by the word of God and prayer.** *(1 Timothy 4:1-5, KJV)*

> *For bodily exercise profiteth little: but godliness is profitable* **unto all things,** *having promise of* **the life that now is,** *and of that which is to come. This is a faithful saying and worthy of all acceptation…*. **These things command and teach.** *(1 Timothy 4:8-9, 11, KJV)*

Once again, this covers both sides of the same coin, the Judaizers and the Gnostics. Both wishing to put restrictions on what to enjoy and be thankful for to the abundant God we can now call Father. We are to enjoy life without the heavy yoke of religion (restrictions). We are to interact with the physical world and enjoy those things the Heavenly Father provides for us, but not to be entangled or ruled by them. That is the key. It is by the restrictions that we become entangled.

The Father created us and wants us to enjoy life. The only catch 22 is to love one another in its truest form: the way He loves us. He gave us free will and the power to choose. He is a Father of abundance, and out of all the fruits of the garden, there was only one fruit He forbade

Adam to eat! Walking in the spirit isn't in denying ourselves the pleasures of this world. It is in fact embracing them with thankfulness and gratitude within the proper balance. The proper balance is that we do all things to God's Glory. The imbalance comes from the misperception gained from Adam eating the fruit. His eyes were opened to seeing evil and good in everything. It is from a distorted view that the things of this earth can rule us. Therein lies its power. So, if I eat a piece of bacon based on human wisdom, with preconceptions about the outcome, it is a bad thing. But, if I eat it in His freedom, then it is good.

All things that He created in the garden were good. He looked and saw it was good. When Eve was eating other fruits, her thoughts weren't, "If I eat this one, I'll become fat. Ahhh! If I eat this one it has too much cholesterol, so my arteries will get clogged." Those thoughts were non-existent. Those thoughts come from our human wisdom not God's.

We are taught what we perceive as being good food and what we perceive as being bad. Give a baby a piece of cake. That baby doesn't know that it contains things that are presumably unfit for consumption. How do we know it? Based on our human experience.

When do things become bad? When am I stepping over the line in enjoying the abundances given of the Loving Heavenly Father? When I give credit to that substance for providing me with my needs. When I'm eating cake as a comfort food instead of relying on Our Comforter, Holy Spirit. When I give credit to a food for giving me a healthy body.

When I think that food is the key to maintaining my health. That is when we overstep.

It does work both ways. Whenever I give a physical substance that is neither good nor evil power over me, give it the credit in providing for my needs, when depressed and I sit and eat a pound of bacon to feel better, etc., then that is my god. If I enjoy three strips of bacon a day, develop clogged arteries, then condemn myself and blame the bacon for my health condition, guess what? I still placed it as a god. We use medicine the same way, a pain pill takes away the pain. Jesus didn't provide our healing for us at the cross. Rather, a physical substance took the pain away. Oops! I got excited and digressed just a bit.

In summary, let's start with the command to abstain from certain foods. Everywhere we turn, we are told to eat this, don't eat that. This is bad. That is good. We get it from the secular world. We get it from other believers, and leaders in the body of Christ. We get it from health professionals. We are constantly bombarded with this on all sides. Does that sound like a doctrine of the devil to you? Do you see how widespread this is? We don't even realize it. We've become hardened to it. I challenge you to name one food that someone somewhere won't say is bad for you. Why does Paul say it is a doctrine of the devil? Because we are calling something that God created for us bad.

Before you say it, all things are made from something that God originally provided for us. I don't care what it is. Sugar? Yup. Potato chips? Yup. Ice cream? Yup. it doesn't matter how you rationalize it. God provided for us the original product. We don't create it. We make it from something He created.

This is where someone will make the point (I've heard people say this), "What about poison ivy, rat poison or cyanide?" So therefore, not all things are consumable. They use this argument to try to prove a point because they lack any scriptural evidence that the food laws of Moses no longer pertain to us and just want to push us into a corner.

My response is simple. I am referring to those things that we currently view as consumable. I'm not going there with this book. I am not going to tempt someone to do something stupid just to prove a point. There is absolutely no need for anyone to go to that extreme. With that stated:

> **For every creature of God is good, and nothing to be refused, if it be received with thanksgiving: For it is sanctified by the word of God and prayer.** *(1 Timothy 4:4-5, KJV)*

Hopefully, the first six chapters have softened up your thinking, and every person who is reading this book now recognizes the wrong mindset we've had when it comes to things that go in through the mouth. We've set aside our life long experiences, and now, the soil of our heart is tilled, fertilized and prepared for the rest of the book. The key to being prepared for what's in the upcoming chapters is recognizing that we have an unhealthy outlook when it comes to who is responsible for our health.

We think that it is our responsibility, through our diet alone, to take care of our bodies. That, if we're suffering from a disease especially stomach ailments, then it's our fault because we haven't "properly" fed the machine. If we don't properly lube the engine of a car, it breaks down, right? If we fail to keep the engine filled with engine oil, then whose fault is it when the engine blows up? How many sermons have you heard on that?

Maybe, just maybe, it isn't that you haven't failed to put oil in the motor. Could it be that you're just relying on the wrong type of oil to feed the machine? The physical substance of oil is the spiritual representation of who? Holy Spirit is our oil. So, perhaps instead of being reliant on the physical food to fuel our bodies, we should become "weak" and recognize we can't feed our bodies with the right physical substance to maintain our health. But when we are weak and can't do it ourselves. Then, He is strong! We've simply been reliant on the wrong type of food. Perhaps we should become reliant on the Bread of Life to sustain us.

It's ok, keep eating whatever diet you're on. The suggestions made in the upcoming chapters are not contingent upon what you're eating. Nor am I suggesting that you stop taking any medications you're currently on. The information in the remaining chapters will lead you, into peace and truly let you enjoy what you're eating now while renewing your mind. Contemplate, what a relief it will be to not be ruled by fear when you eat!

> *For God hath not given us the spirit of fear; but of power,*
> *and of love, and of a sound mind. (2 Timothy 1:7, KJV)*

8: Majority Rules.
Are you Sure?

Think about this, if the majority of people agree on something, it's probably wrong. I'm talking all people, believers and unbelievers, all agreeing on the same subject. People that eat healthy and people that don't. Ask anyone if what you eat will determine how healthy you are. Ninety-nine-point-nine percent will say, "Yes, it does." That is a scary thought.

There is not even one other subject that I can think of where people can agree except when it comes to food. Narrow that thought down. With all the different beliefs in the body of Christ, one of the few messages that nearly every single person has heard is the message that you are responsible for your health through your diet: The Lord helps those who help themselves. Really? That isn't in the scriptures. The Lord helps those who can't help themselves. Read these scriptures while I kick back and drink some coffee.

When Jesus heard it, he saith unto them, they that are whole have no need of the physician, but they that are sick: I came not to call the righteous, but sinners to repentance. (Mark 2:17, KJV)

And he said unto me, My grace is sufficient for thee: for my strength is made perfect in weakness. Most gladly therefore will I rather glory in my infirmities, that the **power** *of Christ may rest upon me. (2 Corinthians 12:9, KJV)*

The reason why we have so many sick believers is that we rely on food to sustain us, not God. We believe we have the power to maintain our health through food. Therefore, we aren't trusting in him to sustain us.

When it comes to our health, we don't let the power of Christ be upon us because we think we can do it through food. We'll beg Him to help us maintain a "healthy" diet, "Please Lord take away my desire for chocolate." Many times, He will do that. Ask and you shall receive. But we're asking for the wrong thing. The children of Israel, begged God for a king. God granted that. How'd that turn out for Israel?

And the Lord said unto Samuel, Hearken unto the voice of the people in all that they say unto thee: for they have not rejected thee, but they have rejected me, that I should not reign over them. (1 Samuel 8:7, KJV)

Now therefore hearken unto their voice: howbeit yet protest solemnly unto them, and shew them the manner of the king that shall reign over them. (1 Samuel 8:9, KJV)

This scripture proves a number of my points. What the majority of people believe are, most of the time, wrong. God's will isn't always done on Earth. God will grant us things that aren't good for us because we ask Him. What seems good to us most often isn't.

> *All the ways of a man are clean in his own eyes; but the Lord weigheth the spirits. (Proverbs 16:2, KJV)*
>
> *There is a way which seemeth right unto a man, but the end thereof are the ways of death. (Proverbs 14:12, KJV)*

Knowledge is power, especially when it's true knowledge of God. All things are neutral. What happens is based on what we believe. Things of the physical world only have the power over us that we give it based on what we believe.

Proof in point: the placebo effect. Give a person a pill filled with sugar. If that person believes that it is medicine that will cure them, then it does. That should be enough proof of God's truth on health. But we are so reliant on human wisdom that the truth escapes us.

The things of the physical nature are fleeting, they are not permanent. If we rely on those things, then it won't last. The only things that last eternally are the things of God. So, when we seek a physical solution to a physical problem, we will find a physical solution. That solution is only temporary. Embedded within that solution are restrictions.

Human wisdom says that the solution is placing restrictions on yourself or others. Have allergies to gluten, which didn't exist several years ago)? The human answer is to have gluten free food. Diabetes? Add more restrictions. If you're overweight, then a calorie restriction is needed.

The more restrictions we place on ourselves or others, the more power we've given it. Worry, anxiety, all those emotions are fear based. We are then ruled by fear. That, my dearest friends, is the law of sin and death.

> *I find a law, that, when I would do good, evil is present with me. For I delight in the law of God after the inward man: But I see another law in my members, warring against the law of my mind, and bringing me into captivity to the law of sin which is in my members. (Romans 7: 21-23, KJV)*

> *...the law of sin and death. (Romans 8:2, KJV)*

This is why we struggle so much with food, medicine, and the drinks we place ourselves under, the law of sin and death. We look at our fixing our actions with diet. Because we look at eating a certain way as sin, we struggle with it.

The more we categorize food as being either good or bad, the stronger the hold becomes. The potato chip is bad. Therefore, we choose a potato chip over a banana. Bacon is bad. Therefore, we choose bacon over a strawberry. Three thousand calories are perfect. Instead, we choose to stuff our faces all day long. Since our bodies are the temple of the Holy Spirit, therefore, we believe it is a sin to choose a potato chip over a peach. Indeed, it would be bad enough if it were only spiritual leaders saying this. But we have the entire field of medicine placing us under the same restrictions. You want proof that we think this way? As you were reading this, you suddenly had the urge for a potato chip or bacon.

As I've told you, I had the propensity to choose a junk food diet. In fact, I refused to eat chicken for over 25 years. Unknown to myself, it was this very law that was the cause of it. In my conscience, I thought it was because I didn't like the taste. The Lord showed me the real reason was the law of sin and death.

Growing up, my parents went from a diet of pasta to chicken and fish. Then, when I went to the military the diet consisted of chicken and fish. Everyone talks about how healthy chicken is. Therefore, I developed a distaste for chicken.

As I continued learning from Holy Spirit about the power the physical senses have over us, I decided to try chicken once again. I have found that I now love chicken. Alcohol and drugs are the same thing. Both have lost the power they both, at one time, had over me because I now rely on Holy Spirit to supply all my needs.

This is the very same principle that, because we look at our food as a matter of life or death, we've given it that power. Therefore, we are now susceptible to what we put into our mouths. In using human wisdom, we have dug our own graves by our reliance and perception of food. Then, if we are attached to a religious organization that teaches that God's diet is the diet of the Old Covenant, we place ourselves further and further into the pit. Our health then becomes subject to physical substances.

This is why I've spent half of this book showing that all of God's creation is pure and given unto us. As God told Peter, do you dare to call that which I've made clean unclean (paraphrased)? Yet we do that very thing without even thinking about it. It is the same thing as with the Law of Moses, the original commandments given to Moses by God.

> *What shall we say then? Is the law sin? God forbid. Nay, I had not known sin, but by the law: for I had not known lust, except the law had said, Thou shalt not covet. But sin, taking occasion by the commandment, wrought in me all manner of concupiscence. For without the law sin was dead. (Romans 7: 7-8, KJV)*

> *For sin, taking occasion by the commandment, deceived me, and by it slew me. (Romans 7:11, KJV)*

The Law of Moses was good, but sin took advantage of it. Thereby, we became helpless. Thank God for Jesus! Added to that was the burden that men added to that law things that weren't in the original commandments.

Jesus consistently pointed out to the Pharisees, "It is by your traditions that make the Law of God of none effect. (BOOK & VERSE)" We do the same with things that go in the mouth, compounded by giving it the power of life and death through our negative confessions. We as humans have made certain foods as being bad. Therefore, we place ourselves under the law of sin and death. This is why we struggle so much with it. That was never the Father's intention, nor did Jesus ever give the representation that food has the power of life and death over us.

I have many friends in the healing ministry. We've all had and seen countless numbers of miracles. We've seen the dead brought back to life, cancer healed, broken bones restored, Lou Gehrig's disease healed. These are wonderful, loved by Jesus folks whose motto is nothing is impossible for God. We've all seen the impossible. Nevertheless, when it comes to food, in their opinion, we are held accountable for what we put into our bodies. We separate food and put it on a pedestal, in a category all by itself as if Holy Spirit is powerless, because we've put the "wrong" or "right" thing into our body. This is placing people under the law of sin and death without realizing it. I will continue to state this, man's opinion of what is good food and what bad food is based solely off of human experience and the physical senses.

Indeed, these are friends of mine who are not swayed by their physical senses when it comes to praying for a person with horrific medical conditions. They stand in faith in spite of what they see and miracles happen. Yet, they can't fathom that whatever goes into the mouth should not affect our health. Again, it is we who have given food that power.

But that is how ingrained into our core being and society it is that we don't even consider there is a different way of thinking about it. Food or anything that goes into the mouth is neutral. Of itself, it has no power. Just that knowledge and belief will go a long way to helping us in overcoming the power we've given physical substances. This problem goes as far back in human history as Adam, Eve, Cain and Esau. I'll give a scripture to the next thought.

> *There is therefore now no condemnation to them which are in Christ Jesus, who walk not after the flesh, but after the Spirit. (Romans 8:1, KJV)*

No one person is weak or to be blamed for the power we give to food.

It is an effect of the original sin. I thank the Father for Christ! What is important is that we start to make a dent in this belief, that food is so powerful. In fact, I want it to be as clear as crystal, if you have a disease where you are on a food restricted diet, you don't have to change your diet while renewing your mind. If you have food allergies, it is the same. You don't have to put yourself at risk.

What we're really learning is to rely on Holy Spirit, not the diet. You can do that while staying on the diet you are presently on. I really mean that. There is no shame or any insinuation that you are condemned for what you eat. In fact, you will find it easier and easier to stick to your diet because food will have less and less control over you. The same is true for those who have trouble with their weight. When learning to rely on Holy Spirit, no matter the reason you struggle, the struggle will become less and less.

I know what it is like to be controlled by a physical substance for forty-three years of my life. The shame and guilt that we and others put upon us is unbearable. The resistance comes from when a person hears me say, that food is neutral and cannot control my health. They immediately think I'm talking about going hog wild and eating everything in sight. People with *similar* beliefs as mine have misrepresented the truth.

I'm not teaching that the end-goal of this is to eat or consume things in a gluttonous manner. The goal is freedom from being controlled by physical substances. Food and drink were given to us for enjoyment and for fellowshipping, to bring us together as a family and a community. It wasn't given to us to be the cause of worry, fear, or disease. The more we put it in its proper place, the more peace we will maintain, because we will place more reliance on Holy Spirit.

One of the hardest things to learn is how to rely on Holy Spirit for all things. We instead must be weak, so He can be strong for us, so that the power of Christ may rest on us. We use the thought that we do what we can in the physical, then Holy Spirit will come swooping down to rescue us.

That isn't how Jesus operated. He relied on the Father first. Then, action followed. In other words, our error is we look for the physical solution first, then we ask for help from God in implementing that physical solution. Here's some examples:

We have symptoms and go to a doctor. According to the doctor, surgery is needed. We beg God to guide the surgeon's hand instead of recognizing that our healing is available now.

We're overweight. So then, we start counting calories, change our diet, and ask God to help in keeping us on our diet.

Imagine the country is in dire straits. So, we ask God for a president who will change the Laws of this land instead of recognizing Christ is our King, not the president. As shown in Samuel, God doesn't want one man in charge of us. He's our King.

The world's stress is crushing in all around me. I turn to alcohol/food for comfort, instead of Holy Spirit.

We need money. So we scheme, beg, and borrow to get the money.

Many of these things there is nothing wrong with. Nothing's wrong with going to a doctor. Nothing's wrong with voting. Nothing's wrong with eating less. Nothing's wrong with eating better foods. But we should be looking for the spiritual answer first.

The Lord is more than happy, to provide a spiritual solution to a physical problem when we believe He will. Look at Jesus' life. It is full of spiritual solutions to physical problems. When Jesus needed to pay the Romans' taxes, He didn't beg a person for money. He sent Peter to the river to get the coin out of the fish's mouth. Things that we would consider frivolous are not so with the Father and Jesus.

Consider the wedding, where Jesus turned water to wine, a physical problem with a spiritual solution. In all His ways, Jesus used the spiritual solution, not the physical solution. In Christ, we have the same choices, even when it doesn't appear to always be that way.

Expand your thinking. Rely on the Heavenly Father first. We are all on this journey to mature In Christ. This is all about renewing our mind to the mind of Christ. The world at times seems to be screaming louder because we separate the spirit from the physical things. There is always *both* the spiritual solution and physical solution. Which one do we choose?

9: If You're Speaking It, You're Getting It

The formula for learning to rely on Holy Spirit is the same as recognizing and acknowledging your healing. Believe in your heart, expect and recognize improvements, then you will see it manifest, or more correctly, you will be able to acknowledge what you are expecting to happen.

The key is that, since food is such a powerful obstacle, acknowledging your healing will happen along the way as you are knocking food off its pedestal. Hopefully, you are convinced that food is neutral and has no power to affect our health in and of itself. Now is where we take steps to rely on Holy Spirit to make that our reality. This will take a concerted effort in changing the way we think about food. As we do this, then we will see many changes and the supernatural will become more natural because we will be relying more on Holy Spirit and less on the physical senses.

In this chapter, there will be perhaps more scriptures than I have ever used before so that you get these truths seeded into your heart. Did I mention that today I visited my Pastor? Bless his heart! He offered me some coffee, which I accepted, of course. Since it wasn't my freshly roasted coffee, it took my relying on Holy Spirit to drink it! I'm partially joking with just a hint of being serious.

The beliefs of the heart and the words that come out of our mouths work together hand in hand. We can speak the correct words, and nothing will happen unless empowered by the beliefs of the heart. We can speak scriptures all year long. Unless we believe what we're speaking, then we get no benefit from them.

The same is true in reverse. We need to take our thoughts captive and speak truth out loud in order to get these truths to our heart. Faith comes by hearing. Therefore, it is an essential part to cementing heart beliefs.

Changing our thoughts, speaking and hearing ourselves speak truth are all essential in renewing our minds and hearts to the truth. They all work together like three strands of rope being twisted together to make an unbreakable rope. Take away one strand, then the rope isn't as strong, causing it to break under stress.

> Keep thy heart with all diligence; for out of it are the issues of life. (Proverbs 4:23, KJV)

> Trust in the Lord with all thine heart; and lean not unto thine own understanding. In all thy ways acknowledge Him, and he shall direct thy paths. (Proverbs 3:5-6, KJV)

We have leaned on human understanding when it comes to diet. We have failed to acknowledge Him when it comes to our health which is why humanity is having such a health crisis. This points right to a heart issue. What we've looked at as logic and common sense is actually tainted human understanding. Therefore, we must change our heart beliefs.

When there is an issue in life, it's usually because of a wrong belief. First, we must acknowledge the truth, settle it in our thoughts by acknowledging the wrong belief (repentance), renew our mind to the truth, then apply this understanding to our heart.

> *So that thou incline thine ear unto wisdom, and apply thine heart to understanding; (Proverbs 2:2, KJV)*

Let's discuss what the scriptures say about how to have a long life and health. These are only a small amount taken only from one book of the Bible. Jesus had much to say about it as well. The purpose of the book of Proverbs is to receive instruction in wisdom, justice, judgment, and equity.

> *They would none of my counsel: they despised all my reproof. Therefore shall they eat of the fruit of their own way, and be filled with their own devices. (Proverbs 1:30-31, KJV)*

This scripture is here to show us, when it comes to food, we have leaned on our own understanding. Therefore, we have eaten the fruit of our way and been left to our own devices. The consequences are exactly what we expect to happen. We have relied upon ourselves for our health and have fallen short. This is just a friendly reminder as we look at the rest of the verses of how to attain a long life.

Fear of the Lord and Wisdom

> *My son, forget not my law; but let thine heart keep my commandments; For length of days, and long life, and peace, shall they add to thee. (Proverbs 3:1-2, KJV)*

> *Be not wise in thine own eyes: fear the Lord, and depart from evil.* **It shall be health to thy navel, and marrow to thy bones.** *(Proverbs 3:7-8, KJV)*

What isn't faith is sin. Having trust in food over trusting the Lord is therefore evil.

> *Happy is the man that findeth wisdom, and the man that getteth understanding....* **Length of days is in her right hand;** *and in her left hand riches and honour. (Proverbs 3:13, 16, KJV)*

> *She is a* **tree of life** *to them that lay hold upon her: and happy is every one that retaineth her. (Proverbs 3:18, KJV)*

> *Let them not depart from thine eyes; keep them in the midst of thine heart.* **For they are life unto those that find them, and health to all their flesh.** *(Proverbs 4:21-22, KJV)*

> *The fear of the Lord is the beginning of wisdom: and the knowledge of the holy is understanding.* **For by me thy days shall be multiplied, and the years of thy life shall be increased.** *(Proverbs 9:10-11, KJV)*

> *The law of the wise is* **a fountain of life,...** *(Proverbs 13:14, KJV)*

> *Hope deferred maketh the heart sick: but when the desire*

cometh, it is a tree of life. (Proverbs 13:12, KJV)

The fruit of the righteous is a tree of life; *and he that winneth souls is wise. Behold, the righteous shall be recompensed in the earth: much more the wicked and the sinner. (Proverbs 11:30-31, KJV)*

Our righteousness is in Christ. The fruit is produced by Holy Spirit.

Our Words

The mouth of a righteous man is a well of life:... (Proverbs 10:11, KJV)

A man **shall be satisfied with good by the fruit of his mouth:** *and the recompense of man's hands shall be rendered unto him. (Proverbs 12:14, KJV)*

There is that speaketh like the piercings of a sword: but **the tongue of the wise is health.** *(Proverbs 12:18, KJV)*

Heaviness in the heart of man maketh it stoop: but a **good word** *maketh it glad. (Proverbs 12:25, KJV)*

A man shall eat **good by the fruit of his mouth:...** *(Proverbs 13:2, KJV)*

The law of the wise is a fountain of life,... (Proverbs 13:14, KJV)

but a faithful ambassador is health. (Proverbs 13:17, KJV)

A sound heart is the life of the flesh: but envy the rottenness of the bones. (Proverbs 14:30, KJV)

A wholesome tongue is a tree of life: but perverseness therein is a breach in the spirit. (Proverbs 15:4, KJV)

A cheerful look brings joy to the heart; good news makes for good health. (Proverbs 15:30, NLT)

Pleasant words are as an honeycomb, sweet to the soul, and health to the bones. (Proverbs 16:24, KJV)

A merry heart doeth good like a medicine: but a broken spirit drieth the bones. (Proverbs 17:22, KJV)

A man's belly shall be satisfied with the fruit of his mouth; and with the increase of his lips shall he be filled. Death and life are in the power of the tongue: and they that love it shall eat the fruit thereof. (Proverbs 18:20-21, KJV)

Keep in mind these are just a small glimpse of what scriptures say gives us long life and health to our body. Throughout scriptures, the prescription is there for a long life and health. Summing it up is God's Wisdom, Fear of the Lord, and the words that come from our mouths. Fear of God, in other words, is a deep reverence for Our Father. Recognizing He is a loving Father who has already provided for us, our Father does not point to needing food to heal us. He said, I am The Lord your God who heals you. We should look to Him to sustain us, putting Him far above properties that man has assigned to food. His wisdom is far above human wisdom. His wisdom in the book of Proverbs points to the words of our mouth as coming from what we believe to be life or death. Just in the book of Proverbs, there are twelve verses alone that point to our speech. There are many people, when it comes to healing, that teach on the power of our words. Yet, to my knowledge, no one points out how our speech puts us at the mercy of food.

"If I eat that, I'll get fat."

"That child eats too much sugar. That is why he is uncontrollable."

"I'm tired because I haven't eaten all day."

"I ate too much turkey. I have to loosen my belt."

"Watch what you eat or you'll be a diabetic."

"That pork is undercooked. I'm gonna get sick."

"My stomach is upset because that food sat out to long."

"I'm allergic to gluten."

"I'm allergic to dairy products."

"I have food allergies."

"If you eat that, you'll die young."

"Bacon for breakfast will kill you."

Not to mention all the side effects of medicines we hear on commercials or read about. The list above is almost never ending. We think nothing about the power attributed to medicine/food by our own speech.

If we start changing our words to the affirmative choices, that alone will help to promote good health. Of course, we have to believe what we speak. What we believe in our hearts is what wins out. Speaking the good things out and listening to ourselves saying it does help to deposit it into our hearts. Then, we start looking with expectation for the positive change. We have to be real with ourselves. We know when we're truly believing something and when we're not.

You're at the snack machine at work, you've already bought a chocolate bar. You're with a co-worker the words out of your mouth are, "I shouldn't eat this." Then, you've got three choices. You can stay with that statement; You can choose not to eat it and give it away, recognizing that it's lost its power over you; or you can change your words to this chocolate will only do good, Thank you Jesus! Either one of the last two options are good.

If you're a diabetic having trouble sticking to your diet but you want to stick with it, recognize that you have the choice. I enjoy this meal. Therefore, I choose to eat it. This food will do only good, thank you Jesus. You have just plowed right through the law of sin and death. "In Christ I have the freedom to choose what I eat. I choose this diet."

These are just a few examples. The main thing is to know that you do have a choice in the matter. The words you choose should reflect the goal you have. If at some point you want to be free from dietary restrictions, then your words should reflect that.

Stay away from using negative words or in sentences that try to reflect a positive result. Avoid words such as "not," "negative," "bad," "not healthy," and "unhealthy." An example is, "I choose *not* to eat in an *unhealthy* way." Simply put, this will reinforce the negative and have undesired results.

It's the way our brain processes the words that we choose. Using mathematics as an example $-1 + -1 = -2$. Two negatives does not make a positive number. In the above sentence, you've got the word '*not*' which

KNOCKING FOOD OFF ITS PEDESTAL

is a negative word and the prefix *un* which is negative. That will not yield a positive result. In fact, you're making the negative stronger, not weaker. I've heard people declare, "I do not have diabetes." This is the same thing as reinforcing that we do have diabetes. Diabetes and not are words that have a negative connotation. The brain is seeing it as, "I do have diabetes."

Take a moment to think about it. Go out into the world armed with some declarations you can use in everyday situations. Make a list. Write it down. I do suggest actually using a pen and a piece of paper which will help you to remember the list. Ask Holy Spirit to bring the list to your remembrance. This is just one suggestion, to get on the path of renewing your mind to the mind of Christ concerning food or anything neutral that goes into the mouth.

> *...commanding to abstain from meats, which God hath created to be received with thanksgiving of them which believe and know the truth. For every creature of God is good, and nothing to be refused, if it be received with thanksgiving: For it is sanctified by the word of God and prayer. (1 Timothy 4:3-5, KJV)*

Now, here is another suggestion that will take a little more explanation. When I use the words, 'bless your food,' you may skip over it or even think, "What good does that do?" Many Christians will use the words, *"bless you,"* yet, say it in a casual way without realizing the real scope of that word. It becomes just a cute word to show how spiritual we are.

The word sanctified as used in the above scripture is the same way. We use it less often, but it has the same casualness about it. There is no empowerment in using it that way. We barely even recognize the meaning behind the words. My definition where it concerns *For it is sanctified by the word of God and prayer'* is that sanctified means set apart and made holy. Holy then means that there is a change in whatever is sanctified. It's made pure. When we accept Jesus, we then became holy through him. The Holy Spirit then takes up residence and there is a change in our very nature whether we act like it or not. We walk by faith, not by sight. The way I look or appear to be may not be evident, but there is a change.

It's the same way with something that we declare to be sanctified through prayer (or blessing). It is now declared to be good therefore it is. So, when I declare something to be sanctified whether its appearance has changed or not, In Jesus Name, it is made fit (holy) for consumption. Therefore, it can only do good when we believe it is good.

Sacrifices under the Old Covenant had to be completely healthy, without blemish. People would eat the sacrifices. These sacrifices would be declared to be holy and fit as a holy sacrifice to God and good to be consumed. This was a physical representation of Jesus. Now that the perfect sacrifice (Jesus) has been made, we are declared to be holy priests unto the Lord. Therefore, when we declare anything to be sanctified, it is, which means that its physical properties have changed, and belief in that makes it only good. Absorb that into your heart.

We are temples of the Holy Spirit. Therefore, what goes into us is changed by Him to be holy. That is exactly what Paul is saying in that passage. It is your choice to believe it or not to believe it.

The word I choose to use to sanctify what goes in the mouth and people as well is the word bless. Since we are sanctified as priests to the Lord, when I state the word blessing or bless it means that I bestow God's favor on that person or thing. The meaning is even deeper. It means that I am bestowing happiness, favor, good health, all spiritual blessings on that substance or person. It is thereby made and presented to be perfect without blemish. This is what we should be aware of at the dinner table, or anytime we put a substance into our mouth. We are declaring that it is holy and fit for the temple of God. We have all spiritual blessings.

One day at one of my car lots, a Pastor owned the car lot, they were talking about some sick folk and their needs. They all knew my testimony. I stated that, In Jesus Name, I bless them. They stared at me. The owner looked at me and stated, "what good is that going to do?" I was shocked. These were men that used that word often. Whenever I entered that car lot, they would say, "bless you brother."

That instance showed me they put no meaning whatsoever behind the word. No faith or expectation whatsoever was empowered by their usage of the word. I simply stated that the word had meaning when I said it. I blessed the sick person again (who wasn't at the car lot. I didn't even know the person). The next week I went back in he stated that the person's condition had improved.

When we grab a snack, eat at the dinner table, drink a cup of coffee, whatever we're doing, bless it, empowered with the belief that its very properties have changed.

When you pray over a meal, don't just use good sounding words or fancy talk. The longer the blessing of a meal the less effective it is, because you've just lost the true meaning of the word blessing. Especially on very special occasions, we want to get long winded and make it sound good. Instead choose words that aren't just meant to blow hot air around.

Ouch! Oh, don't get offended. I'm just saying, the longer the speech, the more our thoughts wander. Your focus will shift from thinking about what it actually means to bless something , "Oh my gosh! Shut up already! I'm ready for the juicy turkey." Then the meaning and purpose is lost. If that's just me, okay. But c'mon. Admit to it. Make this one act the most important aspect of eating. Turn it into a personal, powerful moment where whatever type of substance, the very properties of it have become good with nothing harmful in it at all.

A word on spiritual blessings, they are not just set aside for heaven. Spiritual blessings are everything that is good now in the physical existence. Spiritual blessings are not separate from the physical world, they aren't passive things separate from the physical. They are active and more powerful than the physical nature of things. We dismiss this thinking that a spiritual blessing is outside of material things a spiritual blessing includes this physical world.

Now unto him that is able to do exceeding abundantly above all that we ask or think, according to the power that worketh in us, (Ephesians 3:20, KJV)

Holy Spirit is the power that is in us, and worketh in us when we walk by faith and not by sight. Knowing He has already approved and granted the desire of our hearts. It is expectation and faith that causes Him to jump into action when we believe we have it before we see it.

10: What Are We Missing From the Lord's Supper?

The Lord's Supper is seldom thought about. Some churches may do this once a month. The Lord said to do this often, yet we seldom do it and, then when done, it is a very religious ceremony robbing it of the intended purpose. Let's take a look at Paul's instructions.

> For I have received of the Lord that which also I delivered unto you, That the lord Jesus the same night in which he was betrayed took bread: And when he had given thanks, he brake it, and said, Take, eat: this is my body, which is broken for you: this do in remembrance of me. After the same manner also he took the cup, when he had supped, saying, This cup is the new testament in my blood: this do ye, as oft as ye drink it, in remembrance of me. For as often as ye eat this bread, and drink this cup, ye do shew the Lord's death till he come. Wherefore whosoever shall eat this bread, and drink this cup of the Lord, unworthily, shall be guilty of the body and blood of the lord. But let a man examine himself, and so let him eat of this bread, and drink of that cup. For he that eateth and drinketh unworthily, eateth and

> *drinketh damnation to himself, not discerning the lord's*
> *body.* **For this cause many are weakly and sickly**
> **among you, and many sleep.** *For if we would judge*
> *ourselves, we should not be judged. But when we are judged,*
> *we are chastened of the Lord, that we should not be*
> *condemned with the world. Wherefore, my brethren, when ye*
> *come together to eat, tarry one for another. And if any man*
> *hunger, let him eat at home; that ye come not together unto*
> *condemnation. And the rest will I set in order when I come.*
> *(1 Corinthians 11:23-34, KJV)*

There is no one that can argue that we have many brothers and sisters who are weak and sickly among us. Many have died from diseases. Therefore, we must look at this scripture with an open heart.

In today's churches, we have a situation that is different than in the Corinthian church. They were coming together often to partake of the Lord's Supper. Yet, they were coming to eat and drink as pagans, just as an average feast. They were not proclaiming the Lord's death and what that meant. The Lord's Supper in that day was a full meal with drink. That was the custom of the early church. Indeed, the original supper of Christ was the same. It wasn't a little cracker with grape juice. It was a celebration.

Nothing was wrong with the feast in itself. What was wrong with it was that there was chaos and people shoving each other, grabbing all they could without thought of the Lord's Body and Blood. His body is for our healing and His Blood was shed so that we can enter into the New Covenant in Christ, as sons of God.

Today, in majority of churches, we have forgotten the Lord's Supper. It is done as an afterthought. With the early church it was a celebration which, if we truly understand what was accomplished on the Cross, we as the modern-day Body of Christ should have a celebration and gratitude. Instead, when it is conducted, it is basically done out of ceremony, not gratitude. And we are not recognizing that His was a sacrifice for our lives. This was meant so there would exist a unity and harmony within the Body of Christ.

In my experience in the modern-day body, that is almost non-existent. Not to mention that we have watered it down to one little wafer and a touch of grape juice. This may last for fifteen minutes to thirty minutes if it's a huge congregation. However, there is an overwhelming apathy when it comes down to The Lord's Supper when it should be a time of brothers, sisters, and children having renewed vitality, health, and a rejuvenating of our inner and outer man. That much is quite clear.

I believe these are the reasons the body of Christ isn't eating and drinking itself into condemnation. Instead, out of apathy, we are gathering up condemnation to ourselves as a whole. The most favorable solution would be that churches recognize this and return to the example that the early church fathers laid out for us.

It is also my contention that there is nothing in scriptures that shows it must be taken within a congregation. I take it within my small family and friends. Another option is taking it as a part of an online community group.

I am going to encourage each person to partake of the Lord's Supper often. It is an integral part of renewing our minds to the mind of Christ, especially during times of health crisis. It is a reminder in many ways that we are to eat of the inheritance that His Sacrifice provided for us.

Partaking of the Lord's Supper can be done at any time. In fact, since my healing, I have done it once a week with my wife as we're eating dinner. It is obvious by Paul's letter that there was no ceremony to it. It is a moment to examine oneself and see if we are relying on the wisdom of the Father or on human wisdom for salvation.

Are we being healed, set free, delivered, saved and made whole by His Body and Blood? Are we trying to do these things by our own devices? Are we renewing our mind to the Love of the Father, sharing the fruit of the Holy Spirit with others through unfeigned (not phony) love? Are we allowing His Holy Spirit to flow into the world through us? These are some of the questions that I ask myself.

Then, as I'm eating the elements (in most cases bread), I am remembering His body was broken from the garden to the cross for my healing and divine health. That it is Him, not me, that took my health upon himself. Then as I drink, I remember that by his blood being poured out. I am able to call myself a son of God. It isn't the elements used that are important, but the purity of the heart that matters.

It is at this point I will encourage those who have been sick to immediately look for improvements, expecting them to be present in the body. For those that would balk for not always using bread and grape/wine, I state that Jesus himself stated that it isn't the physical circumcision of the flesh that is important, but the circumcision of the heart. The same would hold true for celebrating the Lord's Supper. It's not the elements, it is in the remembrance.

I am also of the opinion, though I have no way of proving it, that not only did Paul take the Lord's Supper among believers, but when he was alone as well. I even encourage people to take communion as they are taking their medication. That shifts the focus from medicine as healer to Jesus and His finished work healing.

Do as the Holy Spirit guides you. I have set before you my beliefs in a way that is with deep respect and honor to the Lord. Therefore, I do encourage you to keep The Lord in your remembrance always.

> *Thou wilt keep him in perfect peace, whose mind is stayed on thee: because he trusteth in thee. (Isaiah 26:3, KJV)*

> *For the kingdom of God is not meat and drink; but righteousness, and peace, and joy in the Holy Ghost. (Romans 14:17, KJV)*

This verse really sums it up. We look for these things in food and drink. Our troubles with food, drink, even needing medicine start from not relying on the Holy Spirit to meet our needs, but we look to food for these things. "Well Tony most people do. I don't." I know you think you don't, but no matter what side of the spectrum you're on, we all do to some degree. Here are some examples from both sides of the fence:

Righteousness- We have the personality type that strictly watches their diet, making sure that nothing that is considered bad goes through the lips. This person eats the proper quantities of food. Their thought is that they are taking care of the Temple of the Holy Spirit and, therefore, they are in right standing with God.

The person that is on an unhealthy diet is a person that, perhaps, lives off of fast food. They feel that God is not happy with them, because they aren't taking care of the Temple of the Holy Spirit. Therefore, they are not in right standing with God.

Peace- The healthy eater believes they are at peace because they are taking care of their bodies. It is really a false peace. When something happens to their body, they are left wondering what they did wrong.

The unhealthy eater constantly worries about not eating correctly, wishing they could do better. That worry creates stress in their bodies making them sick.

Joy- The healthy eater takes pride by the fact their diet is regulated. Pride is a type of false joy.

The unhealthy eater is feeling unbalanced. Therefore, they are not content. This can lead to depression and placing themselves under the law of sin and death.

We are all somewhere between the two extremes. The key is, no matter where on the scale you are, to pull the rug out from under the power food has over us by relying on the Holy Spirit for His Righteousness, Peace, and Joy. We recognize food is neutral. Therefore, we turn to trusting that Holy Spirit is giving us, His righteousness, peace, and joy. This is also how we pull the rug out from under the law of sin and death when it comes to food.

If food is neutral, there is no way the law (of sin and death) can sneak in and make us feel condemned and under the power of sin. With that way of thinking our diet will naturally become balanced. We will not feel the urge to go to either extreme. The more food becomes neutral, the more our bodies will maintain a balanced level of energy as well because we aren't looking to our diet to maintain our level of energy. We will start to feel the same every day, once again, because we're relying on Holy Spirit and not on a physical substance. Also, Taking the Lord's Supper often, even if it's on our own, will keep us focused on the right things. What we have in Christ is because of what He's freely given us!

11: Is it Sacrifice of Food That The Lord Desires?

Oh, my golly miss molly! As I'm writing this it is Thanksgiving Day! I have so much to be grateful for. Thank you, Heavenly Father and Jesus. It is my favorite Holiday because it is a reminder of how much the Lord has blessed me. I'm thankful for a ton of things.

Let's kick back for a moment and enjoy a cup of coffee while we make a list of what we're grateful for. Post this list on your refrigerator as a reminder that every person has been blessed by the Lord. This is so ironic. On Thanksgiving Day, the first topic of this chapter is on fasting. I am so laughing right now. Thank you, Jesus, for Turkey! Wait for it. This may shock you.

> *Yet they act so pious! They come to the Temple every day and seem delighted to learn all about me. They act like a righteous nation that would never abandon the laws of its God. They ask me to take action on their behalf, pretending they want to be near me. We have fasted before you! they say.*

Why aren't you impressed? We have been very hard on ourselves, and you don't even notice it! "I will tell you why!" I respond. "It's because you are fasting to please yourselves. Even while you fast, you keep oppressing your workers. What good is fasting when you keep on fighting and quarreling? This kind of fasting will never get you anywhere with me. You humble yourselves by going through the motions of penance, bowing your heads like reeds bending in the wind. You dress in burlap and cover yourselves with ashes. Is this what you call fasting? Do you really think this will please the Lord? (Isaiah 58:2-5, NLT)

Our idea of fasting can be so wrong. We think that the Lord is pleased with us sacrificing for Him. Doing without so we can earn His favor. If you're honest with yourself, in these scriptures, there's at least one thing that strikes a chord with you whether you fast corporately, individually, or don't fast at all.

The first week of the New Year, hundreds of churches go on a corporate fast looking to please God so that he will grant them favor. Many fast for our nation because we believe the U.S. is so wicked. We repent for the nation. Really? Is that even possible? Repentance is an individual thing. We shall answer for ourselves, not for what course of action the government chooses. We think that sacrificing pleases God. It doesn't. Have an open heart here, before you answer my next question.

You hear about someone fasting for forty days. What is your first thought? C'mon, be honest! My first thought used to be "That person is so holy." "What an awesome person of God." If giving up food pleases God, then Jesus wouldn't have fed the crowds. He would have said "Go on home hungry. That'll draw you closer to my Father." *Bear with me cause I'm so setting this up.*

When asked why his disciples didn't fast, Jesus replied because He was with them. That once He left, they would fast. When Christ was crucified, they did indeed fast for three days until He was resurrected. In one of Jesus' first appearances, His action was to fix the disciples breakfast.

There is no requirement to fast in the New Testament. Let's take a look at what The Father (even in the Old Covenant) views as a fast that is acceptable to Him.

> **"No, this is the kind of fasting I want:** *Free those who are wrongly imprisoned; lighten the burden of those who work for you. Let the oppressed go free, and remove the chains that bind people. Share your food with the hungry, and give shelter to the homeless. Give clothes to those who need them, and do not hide from relatives who need your help. Then your salvation will come like the dawn, and your wounds will quickly heal. Your godliness will lead you forward, and the glory of the Lord will protect you from behind. Then when you call, the Lord will answer. 'Yes, I am here,' he will quickly reply. "Remove the heavy yoke of oppression. Stop pointing your finger and spreading vicious rumors! Feed the hungry, and help those in trouble. Then your light will shine out from the darkness, and the darkness around you will be as bright as noon. The Lord will guide you continually, giving you water when you are dry and restoring your strength. You will be like a well-watered garden, like an ever-flowing spring. (Isaiah 58:6-11, NLT)*

Add to that:

And as ye go, preach, saying, the kingdom of heaven is at hand. Heal the sick, cleanse the lepers, raise the dead, cast out devils: freely ye have received, freely give. (Matthew 10:7-8, KJV)

Which for those who might think I'm adding to the Word, I'm not. The above scripture would fall under, "Let the oppressed go free, and remove the chains that bind people." This clearly shows what The Father considers an acceptable fast. Many will argue, many are just plain wrong.

I know many people including myself have condemned themselves for either not finishing a fast to the day they had promised the Lord, or for not fasting. We raise people up for doing a long fast and look at them as if they're better than us. It is simply not true. "Tony, but I fasted for such a such time and the Lord answered my prayers." Yes, because the Lord grants the desires of our hearts and you were expecting to receive. It wasn't because you fasted. It was because by the end of the fast, you were able to recognize what had been available all along.

I want this to be a freeing moment. With the burden of a commanded fast or failed fast lifted away, so is the anxiety and worry that because you haven't done this or that, the Lord is withholding from you. He isn't. When you don't fast for the time you set, He isn't saying, "You broke your promise to me! I lift my hedges of protection from you." Not in the least.

As you see from these scriptures, what He considers a fast is so very different than our ideas of one. We struggle because we place ourselves where the law of sin and death can grab us. Which is why the spirits of the world would like nothing more than for you to continue to think that sacrificing food or anything else is pleasing to the Lord. Come out from under that burden!

Part of the beliefs of gnostics is that finding pleasure in things is wrong and that punishing yourself by not eating food is spiritual. Paul refers to this as 'pious self-denial.' With that said, here is a sudden twist. There are huge benefits to fasting, and yes, The Holy Spirit may ask you to fast! *Now you're scratching your head.*

There is nothing in this world that is inherently evil. It is our belief about it that assigns whether an action or object is good or evil. In other words, it is the belief and motive of the heart that make it evil.

> *Blessed are those who don't feel guilty for doing something they have decided is right. 23 But if you have doubts about whether or not you should eat something, you are sinning if you go ahead and do it. For you are not following your convictions. If you do anything you believe is not right, you are sinning. (Romans 14:22b-23, NLT)*

Sex is not evil. But if I do it in a way that it hurts another person, then based on my motives, it is evil. Having sex with my wife is good, but committing adultery is evil. With that in mind, why would the Lord ask us to fast? What would the proper heart motive be in denying oneself food or anything else? The way I ask that question is actually a wrong way to phrase it. It isn't the act of denying ourselves that He is looking for. It is the act of learning to rely on Holy Spirit to meet our needs. This is huge.

problem is that we see fasting as denying ourselves of a need .stead of seeing it as looking to Holy Spirit to provide for that need. We look to food to provide nourishment for our bodies, so we look at fasting as suffering for God. When we change that around to, "I'm fasting to receive physical nourishment from Holy Spirit, then that is a good thing! Yes, I purposely put it that way.

Proof that He will is, once again, the example of my going six months without food. He was sustaining me, and I didn't realize that at the time. I don't have to suffer when I give up food. It isn't the suffering the Lord takes pleasure in, it is that we are learning to trust and rely on Him alone!

Earlier in the book, I mentioned my failed fasts. Now, let's walk this through. I didn't mention my successful fasts for the purpose of this chapter.

My first experience with fasting was in January 2013, five months after my healing. The church I was attending was doing a twenty-one day fast. The suggested fast was no food, but water and soup was fine. We were warned to be committed to the fast and we were making a promise to God, so if we started it, we had better not break it.

I failed miserably. My fast lasted all of three or four days. The man who was healed from Lou Gehrig's disease and went six months without food, couldn't, out of gratitude, discipline himself enough to go just twenty-one days without food. That is what I thought to myself.

I tried again, this time, only promising God a few days. I failed again. During this, I was still praying for the sick and ministering to them. That has never stopped.

Somewhere along that period of time is when the Holy Spirit took me to the scriptures above about fasting. I felt such a relief. That was such a freeing revelation. Still, through my studies, I found several scriptures that showed that there are benefits to fasting. I wanted those benefits.

> *And when they had ordained them elders in every church, and had prayed with fasting, they commended them to the Lord, on whom they believed. (Acts 14:23, KJV)*

> *As they ministered to the Lord, and fasted, the Holy Ghost said,... (Acts 13:2, KJV)*

By these few scriptures, I knew there were benefits to be attained by fasting. The Lord put it in my heart that, this time, fasting wasn't to deprive myself. It was to get closer to Him. To hear Him clearer. I was no longer fasting to get His approval. I was fasting to draw closer to Holy Spirit.

What I had set to be a three day fast turned into seven days. There were a lot of personal revelations in those seven days. It ended suddenly because my wife cooked a pizza. There was no guilt or shame.

My wife cautioned me to come off the fast slowly. My thoughts went to the day of my healing where, after six months of nothing, I ate at Cracker Barrel a full plate of food without any negative effects. I ate the whole pizza and was fine.

The full revelation of this did not strike me at that time. There were lots of short fasts ten days or less. I think, subtly, the full revelation was there underneath my conscious thoughts. I wasn't losing weight or getting weak, light headed, or dizzy even on a ten day fast. But I hadn't put it all together yet.

When fasting, I had stopped making a time limit or even a goal in the number of days that they would last. They would just end when they ended. Then came the time when I fasted for thirty without food or water. Of course, I had no clue that it was gonna turn out that way. In fact, I really wasn't even aware consciously that I was going without water.

It was around day twelve that I was so weak, that I just flopped on the floor and couldn't get up. I cried out to Holy Spirit to give me strength. My wife wanted me to give up the fast. I told this story in an earlier chapter.

All of the sudden, I had strength and clarity of mind. This, I believe, is where I started to put it all together. We don't have to suffer physically even during a prolonged fast. This is how I was learning how to rely on Holy Spirit instead of the world's wisdom. Whenever I would get dizzy or weak, I would cry out to the Holy Spirit, which as time went on, I learned we don't even have to do that. We just have to acknowledge that He's already supplying us with our needs.

I wanted to stay in that moment. So, the fast continued for the thirty days. Once again, I was going to enjoy food. I went and bought a steak and a pizza. I ate the steak and three or four pieces of pizza with my wife telling me I was gonna get sick. I didn't.

This was just the first step in learning what I have about not walking by sight, but by faith. The way I put it is 'relying on Holy Spirit, not on the wisdom of this world or my physical senses.'

Fasting has taught me how to accept the Peace of the Holy Spirit when I start stressing, healing when it's needed, all the things of God. To walk more and more by His Spirit and less and less, by what earthly wisdom says.

It doesn't happen overnight, I've struggled the same as everyone else. I've done it, which means you can to. Your path to this revelation can in fact, come easier than it has for me because of what I'm sharing with you. There are different ways to learn this as well. For instance, if you're on a strict diet and can't fast safely, that's ok. There are other ways that you can learn to rely on Holy Spirit.

An example of this would be that I do not like bathing in cold water. So, If I couldn't fast from food, then another option would be to fast from using hot water while I bathe. Coffee would be another option for me, which I have in fact done. For myself, food is best, but other examples were needed for those who can't fast safely from food. That is, for the moment you may not be able to, but as you learn to rely on Holy Spirit, things will change.

I've only mentioned relying on Holy Spirit during fasting that is just one aspect of it. Indeed, through fasting I learned how to rely on Holy Spirit. But it is far more than that. My singular purpose in fasting is to focus more deeply on relationship with The Father, Jesus, and Holy Spirit. It is a time for me to push all other thoughts aside and get a deeper understanding of my relationship with them. It involves worshipping, praising, studying scriptures more intensely, and of course, speaking in tongues. A lot of the time it gets to be so intense that there may be days without sleep.

It is not something we have to do. Yet, it can become something that we're desiring to do. If it becomes a chore, then the law of sin and death is working. Change your perspective on it.

Do you realize worship is far more than singing? I can be worshiping the Lord while being quiet. That is another revelation that came about during fasting. Studying scriptures, I found there are many ways to do this.

For example, I have read the entire bible out loud one time, and the New Testament four times and counting. Faith comes by hearing, so by reading out loud, we are hearing ourselves speak it. Then, it gets tucked away into our hearts. As I'm looking, hearing, and thinking on the words that are spoken, thoughts start forming. It becomes excitement in studying the word and embracing the imagination, especially with the Old Testament, the Gospels, and the book of Acts. This births new revelations and causes the renewing of the mind. Then, I ask Holy Spirit to guide my imagination, to put the images He wants me to see into my thoughts. This becomes a flow while studying that will have me deep in thought for hours and hours.

Another way of studying scriptures is to speak in tongues while studying. I have found little need for a concordance, although, I will use a concordance from time to time. I have found through speaking in tongues while studying, the true meaning of the words is just deposited into my soul. I have checked this out through looking at other versions of the Bible and through spot checking with a concordance. It is truly amazing.

Having personal revelations is a key to staying on fire for the Lord. The heart stays yearning for more and there is a deep burning that continues as long as we feed it. We feed it through personal study. In fact, it has occurred to me while writing this book, that this year, I've had fewer revelations because the Lord has had me so concentrated on writing books. I want to encourage the reader to try these suggestions out. That they will be just as fruitful for you as they have been for me.

Often times, people will state that while trying to read the bible they become drowsy. They will say that it's the enemy (devil) putting sleep onto them. I have come to the conclusion that it is an enemy: the law of sin and death, not necessarily the devil.

Often, we feel obligated to read the Word. Since we feel obligated, then we open the door to this particular law of the world. Try some of the above suggestions and see if the burning to learn more fires up from deep within. A deeper understanding and relationship will develop.

There have been many times that I've been tired, ready to go to bed. Then, I start studying the Word, and before I realize it, the early morning has come. Where it comes to struggles, most often it is the law of sin and death at work. The way to combat it is by changing your perspective on it.

This leads us right into dying to self. *Get ready to make a huge leap. For many of you, this will be like jumping the Grand Canyon without a motorcycle.*

What is a god? Be warned! This is my definition. A god is a substance or being that has the power and control over life and death.

What is an idol? An idol is something that we place into a position as being a god. Is food therefore an idol? Yes! Can food be an idol and, therefore, a lust of the flesh? Yes! Do we place food as above God? (*I am intentionally shoving you into a corner so that you will be open to what is coming up next.*) You're going to say no.

Why do we avoid things? Out of fear because we believe they have the power to harm or to kill the mortal body. Do you avoid certain foods? You're not allowed to take the cop out answer which is, "Because I don't like it." I will guarantee everyone has any number of foods that they avoid out of fear. The answer is, therefore, yes. If we fear an idol, then isn't that putting it above God (no answer required)?

> *What shall we then say to these things? If God be for us, who can be against us? (Romans 8:31, KJV)*

Is food against us? Food causes high cholesterol, heart attacks, diabetes, liver disease, kidney disease, etc. That would be the truthful answer. Therefore, we do place it above God. Now, you're ready for the next scriptures. Since food can be an idol, therefore, it is contained within the following verses.

> *For whosoever will save his life shall lose it: but whosoever will lose his life for my sake, the same shall save it. (Luke 9:24, KJV)*

> *Mortify therefore your members which are upon the earth; fornication, uncleanness, inordinate affection, evil concupiscence, and covetousness, which is idolatry: (Colossians 3:5, KJV)*

> *That ye put off concerning the former conversation the old man, which is corrupt according to the deceitful lusts; And be renewed in the spirit of your mind; And that ye put on the new man, which after God is created in righteousness and true holiness. (Ephesians 4:22-24, KJV)*

> *Likewise reckon ye also yourselves to be dead indeed unto sin, but alive unto God through Jesus Christ Our Lord. (Romans 6:11, KJV)*

We look to save our lives by diet, not by trusting God. Thereby, if I lose my life through trusting in the Name of Jesus and His finished work, so be it. We are too sensitive to what our bodies are screaming. We are trying to save our lives by trusting in food to keep us healthy. This is not to God's Glory. Yet, we teach, preach and live as if it is.

Once again, food is a neutral substance. It's the position that we put it in that is wrong. Part of dying to self is, as the rest of these verses state, putting off the old man who was controlled by what goes in the mouth and being renewed in the spirit of our minds. Part of dying to self is not being controlled by physical substances to either extreme. In knocking this giant off its pedestal, all the other giants in our lives fall easily.

> *I am crucified with Christ: nevertheless I live; yet not I, but Christ liveth in me: and the life which I now live in the flesh I live by the faith of the Son of God, who loved me, and gave his life for me. (Galatians 2:20, KJV)*

Since I am crucified with Christ and resurrected with Him, with the new man, I am neither better off nor worse off by what goes in through the mouth for He is King of all. This is a lifelong process of learning this. With each step forward, we learn how to truly put our Trust in Him. It will take time and effort. But the more we rely on Holy Spirit, the more we renew our mind day by day, the more true freedom we will walk in. Then, as you enjoy a meal with your family or at a social gathering, others will be amazed at the outpouring of life coming from the Holy Spirit through you. Supernatural health will flow out of you into others.

12: Pray Always

The biggest thing lacking among believers is speaking in tongues. There is as much misteaching in the body of Christ as there is about nearly every doctrine. We're not going to cover this in detail, but enough so that you can see we need it. It is the beginning of the knowledge and wisdom of God. It has been the number one factor in my growing up in Christ so quickly.

After my healing, because I had no teachings on it, I embraced it. The more believers embrace it, the more quickly they will mature, and walk in the fullness stature of Christ. Coffee time! Then, we're going to start at ground zero.

Tongues was first prophesied about through Isaiah.

> *Whom shall he teach knowledge? and whom shall he make
> to understand doctrine? them that are weaned from the milk,
> and drawn from the breasts. For precept must be upon*

> *precept, precept upon precept; line upon line, line upon line;*
> *here a little, and there a little. For with stammering lips and*
> *another tongue will he speak to this people. To whom he*
> *said, This is the rest wherewith ye may cause the weary to*
> *rest; and this is the refreshing: yet they would not hear.*
> *(Isaiah 28:9-12, KJV)*

> *In the law it is written, With men of other tongues and other*
> *lips will I speak unto this people; and yet for all that will*
> *they not hear me, saith the Lord. (1 Corinthians 14:21,*
> *KJV)*

Some scholars will try to say that Isaiah was referencing the
Babylonians. He wasn't. Paul was referencing in this scripture, the
prophecy of Isaiah, which is specifically about speaking in tongues. He
shall teach the knowledge to those that are mature, from stammering
lips and another tongue will he speak to this people. In other words,
God will speak to us through our lips. This is the rest that through this
the weary will find rest and refreshing. We will gain rest through God
speaking through us, which is how he will teach us knowledge so that
we may understand sound wisdom. The rest of the chapter in Isaiah is a
warning, because of aligning this as being of the devil.

> *And these signs shall follow them that believe; In my name*
> *shall they cast out devils; they shall speak with new tongues;*
> *(Mark 16:17, KJV)*

This is a sign to the unbeliever not to the believer. Many people use this
to prove or disprove whether a person is filled with the Holy Ghost.
This is wrong. Tongues is a sign to unbelievers not to other believers.
Therefore, all believers should be speaking in tongues. This is just as
casting out devils and healing are signs to unbelievers and should be a

way of life for believers. On the day of Pentecost, the first thing that happened was speaking in tongues.

> *I have yet many things to say unto you, but ye cannot bear them now. Howbeit when he, the spirit of truth, is come, he will guide you into all truth:... (John 16:12-13, KJV)*

> *And they were all filled with the Holy Ghost, and began to speak with other tongues, as the Spirit gave them utterance. (Acts 2:4, KJV)*

> *And when Paul had laid his hands upon them, the Holy Ghost came on them; and they spake with tongues, and prophesied. (Acts 19:6, KJV)*

> *For they heard them speak with tongues, and magnify God, Then answered Peter, (Acts 10:46, KJV)*

The above verses all show that, as soon as a person accepted Christ, they were baptized with the Holy Ghost and immediately started speaking in tongues. This should be the same today. The problem is the way speaking of tongues is taught and believed. Many believers fear speaking in tongues. Others think it foolish. We can't receive anything if we don't believe. The Holy Spirit forces nothing upon us.

> *But God hath chosen the foolish things of the world to confound the wise; and God hath chosen the weak things of the world to confound the things which are mighty; (1 Corinthians 1:27, KJV)*

People get confused and misteach tongues because they misinterpret Chapter fourteen of 1 Corinthians. There are three main categories: speaking to God, tongues of angels, and tongues of men.

Though I speak with the tongues of men and of angels… (1 Corinthians 13:1, KJV)

Tongues of men is speaking in another person's language that is unknown to you, such as on the day of Pentecost. The tongues of angels are varied, but the most common usage to my understanding is as a message. For instance, there is the gift of speaking in tongues, which in chapter 14, Paul is speaking specifically about and laying down guidelines for use in church. This is what confuses people into thinking that tongues are only while at church and only given to certain people. The best is last, tongues, to God. This is praying in the spirit, or as I refer to it, our private prayer language. This is the type of tongues we're going to concentrate on as individually, this is the type that is crucial in our daily lives.

In chapter 14, Paul is setting the groundwork and is referring to a church setting. Since in that day and age they started speaking in tongues immediately, Paul doesn't have to teach them about tongues as a private prayer language, but he did have to teach them the proper usages.

*Follow after charity, and desire spiritual gifts, but rather that ye may prophesy. For he that speaketh in an unknown tongue **speaketh not unto men, but unto God**: for no man understandeth him; **howbeit in the spirit he speaketh mysteries**. But he that prophesieth speaketh unto men to edification, and exhortation, and comfort. He that speaketh in an **unknown tongue edifieth himself**; but he that prophesieth edifieth the church. **I would that ye all spake with tongues**, but rather that ye prophesied: for greater is he that prophesieth than he*

> *that speaketh with tongues, except he interpret, that the*
> *church may receive edifying. (1 Corinthians 14:1-5, KJV)*

The whole reason for gathering together is for each other, to edify, exhort and comfort. Therefore, if you are speaking in tongues in front of the congregation without interpretation there is no benefit to the body of Christ. But he points out the benefits of tongues as a personal prayer language.

> *I thank my God, I speak with tongues more than ye all: Yet*
> *in the church I had rather speak five words with my*
> *understanding, that by my voice I might teach others also,*
> *than ten thousand words in an unknown tongue. (1*
> *Corinthians 14:18-19, KJV)*

Once again, this scripture shows Paul clearly using tongues as a private prayer language to edify himself in his inner man. **Yet,** in a church setting he would rather speak the common language to edify all in attendance.

> *But if there be no interpreter, let him keep silence in the*
> *church; and let him speak to himself, and to God. (1*
> *Corinthians 14:28, KJV)*

In this scripture, Paul isn't even saying to not speak in tongues if there is no interpreter. Rather, just speak it silently that you may be edified. See how clear the separation is? Yet, many bad theologies come from this.

> *Wherefore, brethren, covet to prophesy, and forbid not to*
> *speak with tongues. (1 Corinthians 14:39, KJV)*

There are many scriptures fully supporting how beneficial using tongues as a private prayer language is. As you saw from the above, by speaking in tongues you are praising God, speaking to God, building up the inner man, and having mysteries revealed unto you. All these things shall be added unto you through the use of tongues as a private prayer language. Now, for a few of many scriptures that do indeed tell us to pray this way:

> *Likewise the Spirit also helpeth our infirmities: for we know not what we should pray for as we ought: but the spirit itself maketh intercession for us with groanings which cannot be uttered. (Romans 8:26, KJV)*

This is for us, with groanings which cannot be uttered. This scripture actually means groanings which cannot be expressed with known words. We are to speak them.

> *Praying always with all prayer and supplication in the Spirit, and watching thereunto with all perseverance and supplication for all saints; (Ephesians 6:18, KJV)*

> *But ye, beloved, building, up yourselves on your most holy faith, praying in the Holy Ghost, (Jude 1:20, KJV)*

There is also a teaching that tells people that the Holy Spirit will force us to speak in tongues and that we cannot control it. This is not true. We can stop and start speaking in tongues as we desire. We have to open our mouths and engage our vocal cords. Holy Spirit will not do it for us. Though once you start speaking in tongues, the desire may become so strong that you will almost feel like you can't stop. Trust me, been there. In which case, if the situation is favorable, then I won't stop speaking in tongues. This is how I learned to speak in tongues: in silence, without being vocal so I could continue speaking in tongues even in public places.

> *And the spirits of the prophets are subject to the prophets. (1 Corinthians 14:32, KJV)*

The word prophet here is a general term meaning any person. This chapter, once again, is for your general knowledge, to get you encouraged to start speaking in tongues. Just by taking the plunge into this, it will increase your faith and expectation into the things of Christ. It will also guide you into being able to easier acknowledge healing because it requires the same steps: believe, expect, and then see it happen. The kingdom of God operates in this way in every facet of living in the kingdom. You must believe it before you can see it or acknowledge it. We walk by faith, not by sight. Therefore, we believe it to see it.

Do your own study on tongues without any preconceived notions. Then, you shall be led into the truth of it. Do not be swayed by man's opinions, but be swayed by the Holy Spirit.

The way to get started is not to wait. When we received the Holy Spirit, we received all He has to offer. As previously shown, the early church was immediately baptized in the Holy Spirit and spoke in tongues immediately upon receiving. Impressions in the inner man will bubble up, engage your vocal cords, and just let those impressions flow out. It does not matter what it is. Just do it.

Your thoughts may say that you're making the sounds up. You are not.

Take those thoughts captive and continue speaking it out. In fact, there is a scientific study out that shows that, when a believer is speaking in tongues, the part of the brain that is used in speaking is not engaged at all. Therefore, it is not you making it up. According to this study, it is an impossibility that one can make it up.

Look this up on the internet. It is your choice to believe it or not. After all, anyone can find a study that supports their point of view. Do you want all that being In Christ has to offer? If so, believe it in spite of what human logic would tell you. God doesn't need you or me to use human logic or human reasoning or human common sense. He gave us a sound mind which is the mind of Christ.

The things of God are not always logical. Just look at the Bible. There are hundreds of circumstances that are not logical to the human mind. Facing a giant as a child is not logical. Facing an army of thousands with three hundred men is not logical. Feeding thousands with just a few fishes and bread is not logical. Touching a cloth to be healed is not logical. The kingdom of God is not always logical to the human mind.

So, go into a room by yourself, engage your vocal cords, and take it by faith that it is Holy Spirit in you. Then, you will reap supernatural benefits from doing so. You can also grab a person who speaks in tongues, listen to them, and mimic them. That will help to jump start you, as well.

13: Landing the Plane

My friends, this journey is about complete. As always, it's been an adventure. I'm crying right now as I always do. Tears are running down my cheeks. What else can I say? Let's take a moment as I drink some coffee and ask Holy Spirit for some final words that will deposit some more wisdom into your person.

> *The fear of the Lord is the beginning of knowledge:...*
> *(Proverbs 1:7 KJV)*

When we gain the fear of the Lord, then we realize He in us is more powerful than any physical substance. After he had created all things, he looked and saw that it was good. That has never changed. He created all things to be good and with no evil having a part of it.

It is mankind with the accusing spirit of the world that caused us to see evil in his creations. It is in the recognition of this that we obtain His viewpoints on these matters. As we learn to separate human wisdom from Godly Wisdom, we eat the fruits of seeing His goodness in all things. Then fear of anything else can no longer influence us. Fear has then lost its hold on us and we achieve a greater freedom than was ever known before. With true freedom comes a balance. We are no longer under influence of a physical substance which means that the physical substance has lost control over us. Therefore, it can no longer negatively influence us. It becomes unimportant, allowing us to focus on the goodness of a Loving Father and sharing that goodness with others.

Remember, living in the spirit is a separate, personal path for each person. He will guide you. The solutions that I've offered in this book are the path the Lord took me on. The key is to believe the truth that is unchangeable.

I believe the most important aspect of this book is in the first seven chapters. These chapters hopefully have given you a different perception that will nudge you in the right direction. Then, because of the change in perception, you will be open to what the Holy Spirit has been telling you all along that you just couldn't hear at the time. In fact, when telling friends about this book, they've told me that Holy Spirit has been guiding them down the same path. This is so encouraging.

As I'm giving my final thoughts, what applies to food and drink applies to medicine as well. Medicine is just like food, neutral when we believe that. My recommendation is the same as food. Keep taking it, but switch your focus to its Holy Spirit that is taking the symptoms away, lowering your blood pressure, whatever the circumstance is. Bless the medicine while changing your expectation from its the medicine to its Holy Spirit. While blessing your medicine, it is helpful to speak that there will be no side-effects from the medicine itself. That it shall do only good and no harm.

With people that are undergoing chemo or radiation, I do the same thing. I speak that those treatments will do no harm to the body. I've gotten a lot of testimonies back that they went through the treatments with no ill effects at all.

Renewing your mind to this can be a process. The more you change your thought process and what you place your expectation on, the quicker you'll see changes. One fella I actually never talked to personally, but left him a message on his phone. About two months later, a friend delivered to me the fellas mri which showed the cancer was gone. Yet, he had suffered no side effects from the intense chemotherapy they had him on. Trust and rely on Holy Spirit absolutely, but listen to the doctors as you are renewing your mind.

Before I came to Christ, before my healing, food utterly controlled me as well as drugs and alcohol. As I've matured in Christ, whatever has gone through my mouth has had less and less control. Sure, I did have the fact that I survived without food for so long. But through the beginning stages, that hadn't even crossed my mind. It wasn't until I started writing, "The Lord Jesus Healed Me" in 2016 that the full impact of that miracle actually became revelation. My point is that it doesn't require a miracle as big as that to start on the right path.

In starting down this path though, bigger miracles than that can occur in your life. Take out the giant and those smaller than the giant will fall more easily. As your perception is switched from the physical things to Christ, these lesser things will fall. As you change your mind from it's the medicine helping to ease the pain to it's Holy Spirit in me giving life to my body, things will fall off of you to where a doctor will say that you no longer need that medication, or you'll come to the realization on your own.

Trusting in the Father, Holy Spirit, and the finished work of Jesus is the only thing worthy of your trust. Learn to grow that trust and increase your expectation. With each victory, relish it, recognize how big each little step is.

I'll never forget a time where I had travelled to meet a person. She had been struggling with throat cancer. The cancer was healed, but she was struggling with eating normally. We talked, and I prayed over her for an hour or two. All of the sudden, she said "I'm going to eat a chicken sandwich now." This was something she couldn't have eaten before. She shoved that sandwich down her throat so fast, I hadn't even had time to finish my cup of coffee. She was perfectly fine! Thank you, Jesus. She did not need any suggestions from me. The Holy Spirit put that desire in her heart.

A dear friend of mine was allergic to almonds. One day (I think absentmindedly), she popped them into her mouth. There was no allergic reaction! It was just a Holy Spirit set-up.

Another friend who I'd been teaching for a year or so one day decided to eat a chicken sandwich (I don't know what it is involving chicken sandwiches). She could eat chicken alone but not on a bun. She ate it with no problem .

As I'm writing this, I'm remembering more and more people that I've taught that, without me saying a word, have just overcome food allergies and strict diets. Most of the time, they hadn't even fully grasped my message on food. In fact, I don't know that I've ever been as in-depth as I've been in this book. Yet, without saying a word to them the Holy Spirit had arranged to show them that they were in fact healed.

That is how I can confidently state that you do not have to even have a plan on changing your diet. It will naturally happen through Holy Spirit. It isn't the diet that's even important, it's just your perception on food that will change things.

When you place Holy Spirit above food, then food has to bow its knee. Medicine is the same way. Just by a perception change so many people have been told by a doctor they no longer need blood pressure medicine, diabetes medicine, pain pills, etc. ....

It seems like I always end my books on the days that I've got to do some grocery shopping. May the Lord grant you all the desires of your heart and maybe we'll meet while I'm out and about.

Be blessed, Be healed, and be a blessing.

Hey! Do me a favor, right now! See Holy Spirit giving life to your body. Move around with eager anticipation that you *will* recognize improvement. That pain you experienced before is gone. The body part that wouldn't move before is moving. The kidney that was functioning less than perfectly is now in perfect condition. Thank you, Jesus! Now get out there! Live a vibrant and healthy life. Pray for others and see them healed. Be a light where it is needed the most. Will you do that for me? Please drop me an email with any testimonies that you have. I look forward to hearing from you. An Amazon Review will also be extremely helpful. Remember that you are loved by myself and, more importantly, by The Father, Jesus, and Holy Spirit.

I'm off to do some grocery shopping which I totally despise. Maybe we'll meet there, and you can do my shopping for me! *Be Blessed, Be Healed, and Be a Blessing! Much Love, my friends.*

About the Author

Tony Myers is author of the books "The Lord Jesus Healed Me" and "Unlocking the Mystery of Diving Healing." He lives in Virginia with his precious wife Deb and all their four-legged family members. A former atheist who was healed from Lou Gehrig's disease, this illness left him paralyzed and dying. Then, he was suddenly healed by Christ.

Since his healing on July 4th, 2012; He has appeared as a guest on many different platforms and media. This includes radio, television, and of course the internet. Most of his time is spent on his business and ministering the Gospel of Christ to others. The planned future holds more speaking engagements and more books to come. Tony is very open to be contacted for prayer, ministry, book signings, and for opportunities to preach the Gospel of Christ.

Check out his website tonybelieves.com,

Facebook @tonyjustbelieves or

Email: tonyjustbelieves@gmail.com

More from Tony

After living a life of atheism, Tony Myers was fighting for his life. He was completely paralyzed, and his body was shutting down. Diagnosed with Lou Gehrig's disease, a debilitating neurological disease with no cure or treatment options, all hope was lost. Then suddenly one day, Tony, determined to end his own life, found a miracle healing instead!

During this journey you will cry, laugh, feel his wife's heartache, and then finally have a tremendous burst of joy as you celebrate his miracle with him and his wife Deb. Tony's honest, folksy telling of his story will make you believe he's sitting right in front of you drinking coffee! This story will encourage, motivate, and inspire you to believe in a miracle for yourself. If you are need of hope and encouragement, then this book is for you.

This book is the field manual as far as receiving healing for yourself is concerned. It is meant to awaken in the readers the mind of Christ and help them tap into the God-realm (i.e., "kingdom of heaven"). That's where we can receive the riches of Christ provided to us by grace. specifically, divine health and healing.

60401316R00090

Made in the USA
Columbia, SC
14 June 2019

Divine healing from the comfort of your home? Is that truly possible?

The problem isn't getting new information. The problem is getting what's already available to work for you. Over many centuries, the simple message of the cross has been obscured and diluted by many religious and secular traditions. And that's exactly why and where this book comes in. Its purpose is to get you to see the simple truth of the Gospel as it's related to divine healing and health, without any unnecessary additives. This book is written in a simple, conversational style. It takes you from the garden of Eden all the way to the present day. It shows you how the revelation about divine healing and health was offered by God, and how and why it kept on getting ignored and put aside. Most importantly, this book shows you what you can do to recover God's blueprint for your own health and how you can get the Gospel truth about divine healing to work for you from the comfort of your home.

Before you close this book, please go to amazon and leave a review. Thank you very much!